WORLD
HUMANITARIAN
DATA AND TRENDS
2015

OCHA

Introduction

World Humanitarian Data and Trends presents global- and country-level data-and-trend analysis about humanitarian crises and assistance. Its purpose is to consolidate this information and present it in an accessible way, providing policymakers, researchers and humanitarian practitioners with an evidence base to support humanitarian policy decisions and provide context for operational decisions.

The information presented covers two main areas: humanitarian needs and assistance in 2014, and humanitarian trends, challenges and opportunities. This edition also features a new section on regional perspectives, which showcases region-specific trends identified by OCHA's regional offices. The report intends to provide a comprehensive picture of the global humanitarian landscape, and to highlight major trends in the nature of humanitarian crises, their drivers, and the actors that participate in prevention, response and recovery. The 2015 edition builds on previous iterations of the report, providing an overview of 2014 as well as selected case studies that can be used for humanitarian advocacy.

There are many gaps in the available information due to the complexity of humanitarian crises. Even the concepts of humanitarian needs and assistance are flexible. There are also inherent biases in the information. For example, assistance provided by communities and by local and national Governments is less likely to be reported. The outcomes and impact of assistance are difficult to measure and rarely reported. Funding data is more available than other types of information. There are also limitations on the availability and quality of data. Further information on limitations is provided in the 'User's Guide'.

The data presented in this report is from a variety of source organizations with the mandate, resources and expertise to collect and compile relevant data, as well as OCHA-managed processes and tools, such as the inter-agency appeal process and the Financial Tracking Service (FTS). All the data presented in this report is publicly available through the source organizations and through the report's own data set. Further information on data sources is provided in the 'User's Guide'.

World Humanitarian Data and Trends is an initiative of the Policy Analysis and Innovation Section of OCHA's Policy Development and Studies Branch (PDSB). This report is just one part of OCHA's efforts to improve data and analysis on humanitarian situations worldwide and build a humanitarian data community. This edition was developed with internal and external partners, whose contributions are listed in the 'Sources and References' section. OCHA extends its sincere gratitude to all those partners for their time, expertise and contributions.

Interpreting the visuals and data

The report uses many visual representations of humanitarian data and trends. There is also some limited narrative text and analysis, which provides basic orientation and helps to guide individual interpretation. However, there may be multiple ways to interpret the same information.

The 'User's Guide' contains more detailed methodological information and specific technical notes for each figure. Readers are encouraged to refer to the technical notes for more detailed descriptions of decisions and assumptions made in presenting the data.

For the latest information on needs and funding requirements for current strategic response plans or inter-agency appeals, see **fts.unocha.org**.

Accessing the data

All the data presented in this report can be downloaded through the Humanitarian Data Exchange (**https://data.hdx.rwlabs.org/**). The report can be explored through its interactive companion microsite **www.unocha.org/humanity360**.

Contents

Highlights[1]

The humanitarian community is doing more, for more people

2014 was a record year on many fronts. The humanitarian community[2] targeted more people than ever before (76 million) and it received more funding than even before ($10.8 billion through inter-agency appeals, $24.5 billion overall). Development indicators (page 52) in the six crises with continuous inter-agency appeals for 10 years or more, such as infant mortality rate and access to improved water sources, have improved as humanitarian spending per person has increased.

However, not all records reached in 2014 had such a positive note. Four inter-agency appeals surpassed the billion-dollar mark (Iraq, South Sudan, the Syria Regional Refugee Response Plan and the Syria Humanitarian Assistance Response Plan), and the majority of funding requested and provided went to these mega-crises. The global funding gap was the largest to date, both in absolute terms ($7 billion) and percentage terms (40 per cent). The amount of funding requested through inter-agency appeals was also a record ($18 billion). Within the context of UN peace operations, humanitarian action became the costliest UN activity ($10 billion), with funding levels surpassing the budget of peacekeeping operations ($8 billion) (page 42).

Last year's report introduced a metric to understand the level of public attention for different crises by calculating the ratio of ReliefWeb reports to web page visits. Using that same metric, it was possible to observe potential cases of donor fatigue and discrepancies with the widely held notion that funding follows public attention (page 8). For example, South Sudan ranked highly in terms of public attention and received high levels of funding. However, Somalia ranked high in attention but its funding levels dropped by two percentage points.

Conflict, the absence of political solutions and vulnerability continued to drive protracted crises

Protracted, conflict-driven emergencies continued to test the humanitarian community's capacity. In total, 59.5 million were displaced by conflict or violence, with an average 30,000 new displacements per day. Between 2011 and 2014, nearly 145,000 deaths and injuries were recorded from the use of explosive weapons; 78 per cent were civilians (page 66). The overall number of people affected by natural disasters or displaced by conflict increased to 200.5 million, more than 50 million compared with 2013.

Global conflict trends were even more dramatic in the Middle East and North Africa region (page 30). This was the only region in the world to experience an increase in high-intensity conflicts, reaching a record 14 in 2014. Further, the number of IDPs in the region more than doubled in five years, from 6.7 million to 15.6 million between 2009 and 2014. In the absence of political solutions, the region's crises are likely to continue affecting the livelihoods, safety and resilience of communities.

Better analysis and new technologies are creating incentives to be more efficient and effective

The humanitarian community continued to innovate and find new ways to work more efficiently and effectively. During the Ebola crisis, digital

---

1 All the information in this section is featured in infographics throughout the report. For specific sources, please refer to the appropriate figure as well as the 'User's Guide'. The most recent year for which complete data is available is 2014. Therefore, this publication is not intended to provide information on the status of current emergencies. Its aim is to track some of the root causes of today's crises and understand the provenance of humanitarian requirements.

2 Humanitarian assistance involves a plethora of actors, from affected people and communities to local and national Governments, civil society and international aid organizations. Organizations account for what they do in varying ways, and the efforts of many actors may not be reported. This publication acknowledges the important contribution of all humanitarian actors, and uses the term 'humanitarian community' to denote those actors that receive international humanitarian funding.

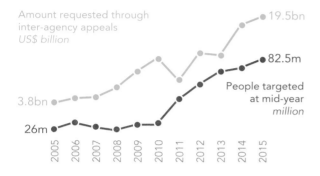

Figure A: Inter-agency appeals: funding requested and people targeted

Amount requested through
inter-agency appeals
US$ billion

19.5bn

3.8bn

82.5m

People targeted
at mid-year
million

26m

2005 2006 2007 2008 2009 2010 2011 2012 2013 2014 2015

humanitarians established a Skype group (page 74) to assist information sharing. The group also facilitated the participation of non-traditional responders. Separately, online volunteers compiled information on healthcare facilities (page 72). The information was then mapped out to provide a comprehensive picture of existing healthcare facilities and released to support responders. Open-source tools, such as KoBoToolbox facilitated assessments by providing a template for data collectors and the capacity to share results in real-time and perform quick analysis. The use of social media to support humanitarian response also evolved: following Typhoon Ruby (page 76) in the Philippines, over 12,000 tweets were categorized to gain information about humanitarian aid, requests for help and locations of damage.

Humanitarians also made headway in building programming based on data analysis: a study of 31 Central Emergency Response Fund (CERF) grants for Haiti and the Asia-Pacific region show that nearly 85 per cent of funding was used to support response in the food, WASH, health, shelter and logistics sector (page 28) This type of insight and analysis will lead to better programming and pre-positioning of supplies.

National Governments further demonstrated their commitment to build their capacity to undertake disaster management capacity. In the Asia-Pacific region, the number of countries with a formal disaster management authority continuously increased since 2006 to reach a record 26. Further, all of the 10 countries that had the highest numbers of disasters and disaster-affected people (page 58) had a formal disaster management authority.

Despite these advances, the humanitarian community continued to experience challenges in truly understanding humanitarian need: measuring impact continues to be a challenge, and the lack of sex and age-disaggregated data makes it difficult to understand the special requirements of women and children in humanitarian situations. Data is patchy: a study of 10 countries in Africa (page 70) showed that at the national level, data was available for a wide range of development indicators (e.g. education, access to drinking water, mobile phone use) but there was barely any information available on disaster risk reduction or gender dimensions.

In May 2016, humanitarians, policy-makers and affected people will meet at the World Humanitarian Summit. This presents a unique opportunity to support a move towards a new humanitarian paradigm – an *Agenda for Humanity* – driven by analysis, based on a full understanding of needs and risks, promoting collective outcomes and shared accountability, and leveraging each other's comparative advantages to truly meet the needs of affected people.

"This year the UN marks its seventieth anniversary. Sadly, there is little time for reflection or celebration. More pressing are the competing demands and challenges fuelled by an upsurge in conflict, disease and human suffering … the international community must rise to the moment."

Ban Ki-moon, **UN Secretary-General, 2015**

THE YEAR IN
REVIEW, 2014

Humanitarian assistance in 2014

In 2014, overall needs and requirements increased, putting even more strain on responders. Notwithstanding current crises, 2014 was a record year on many fronts: funding requirements ($18 billion), overall contributions ($24.5 billion), people targeted (76 million) and a 40 per cent funding gap. The size of the humanitarian community continued to expand: the number of jobs advertised through ReliefWeb and the number of hiring organizations increased by over 3,000 each. There was, however, a slight decrease in the number of organizations participating in inter-agency appeals. On a positive note, the number of incidents affecting aid workers decreased, potentially due to investments in security management.

Affected people

141 million affected people by natural disasters

59.5 million people forcibly displaced by violence and conflict

76 million people targeted by inter-agency appeals

Sources: Aid Worker Security Database, ALNAP, CRED EM-DAT, FTS, OCHA, ReliefWeb, UNHCR

It is still difficult to gauge the impact of international humanitarian assistance. Compounding this challenge, information about national capacities and funding outside of traditional channels is not regularly captured or reported. Assistance is often measured in terms of funding, but this is not an accurate proxy for humanitarian need. Over the last year, there has been increased support for programming based on common risk analysis and more evidence-based decision-making, with platforms such as the Humanitarian Data Exchange facilitating openness and data sharing.

FIGURE 1

Funding

Capacity

26,309 jobs advertised on ReliefWeb

4,480 global number of operational aid agencies

International humanitarian funding
$24.5 billion

4,094 organizations hiring through ReliefWeb

190 aid worker security incidents in 2014

OECD-DAC Donors
$16.8 billion
(represents 10.8% of ODA)

Top three advertised job categories
Number of jobs

329 aid workers affected by security incidents in 2014

Non-DAC Donors
$1.9 billion

Program/Project management 9,345
Monitoring and Evaluation 4,435
Media/Communications 2,446

Private Donors
$5.8 billion

International

667 humanitarian organizations participating in inter-agency appeals

Requirements for consolidated appeals $18 billion

Funding for consolidated appeals $10.8 billion

Per cent covered 60%

Unmet requirements
$7.2 billion

Inter-agency appeals

Humanitarian needs – inter-agency appeals, funding and visibility

In 2014, appeal funding requirements increased by 38 per cent compared with 2013. There have been eight new appeals since 2013, bringing the total to 27 in 2014. There were three level-three emergencies: Central African Republic (CAR), the Philippines (Super Typhoon Haiyan) and Syria. A record number of inter-agency appeals surpassed the billion-dollar mark (Iraq, South Sudan, the Syria Regional Refugee Response Plan and the Syria Humanitarian Assistance Response Plan). The majority of funding requested and provided went to these mega-crises. Iraq, South Sudan and the Syria response plans accounted for approximately 55 per cent of funding required and requested. Globally, the average amount of funding received per person increased by $28 to $182. In 2014, only four per cent of projects were gender-specific, showing no increase from previous years.

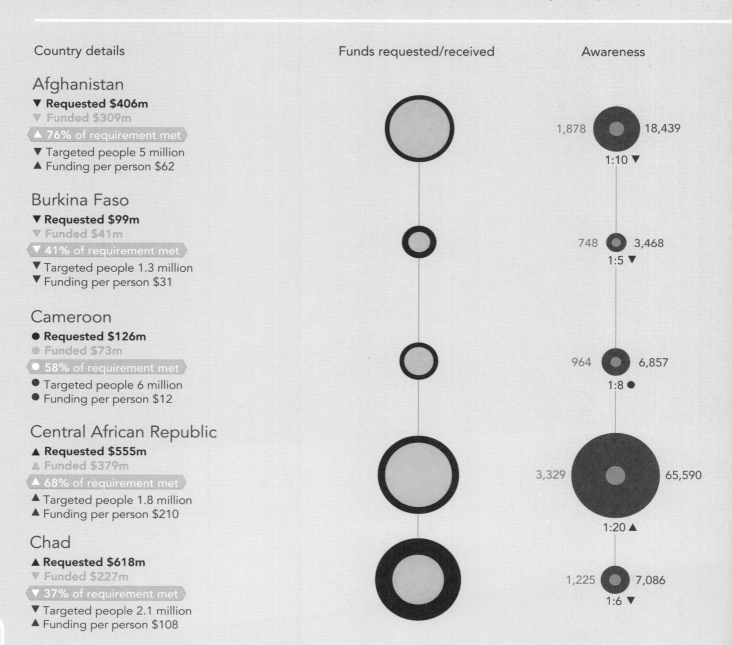

Country details	Funds requested/received	Awareness

Afghanistan
▼ **Requested $406m**
▽ Funded $309m
▲ 76% of requirement met
▼ Targeted people 5 million
▲ Funding per person $62

1,878 · 18,439
1:10 ▼

Burkina Faso
▼ **Requested $99m**
▽ Funded $41m
▼ 41% of requirement met
▼ Targeted people 1.3 million
▼ Funding per person $31

748 · 3,468
1:5 ▼

Cameroon
● **Requested $126m**
● Funded $73m
○ 58% of requirement met
● Targeted people 6 million
● Funding per person $12

964 · 6,857
1:8 ●

Central African Republic
▲ **Requested $555m**
△ Funded $379m
▲ 68% of requirement met
▲ Targeted people 1.8 million
▲ Funding per person $210

3,329 · 65,590
1:20 ▲

Chad
▲ **Requested $618m**
▽ Funded $227m
▼ 37% of requirement met
▼ Targeted people 2.1 million
▲ Funding per person $108

1,225 · 7,086
1:6 ▼

Sources: FTS, inter-agency appeal documents, ReliefWeb, UNHCR

Last year's report introduced a metric to understand the level of public attention for different crises by calculating the ratio of reports to web page visits. Using that same metric, it was possible to observe potential cases of donor fatigue and discrepancies with the widely held notion that funding follows public attention. As with last year, South Sudan ranked highly in attention and funding. However, this was not the case for Somalia. That country continued to rank highly in attention, but its funding level dropped by 2 percentage points. The attention level on Afghanistan dropped by 4 points, but its funding level increased by 2 percentage points. The overall trend shows that while public interest can sometimes be aligned with funding, there is no direct correlation between attention and inter-agency appeal funding.

FIGURE 2

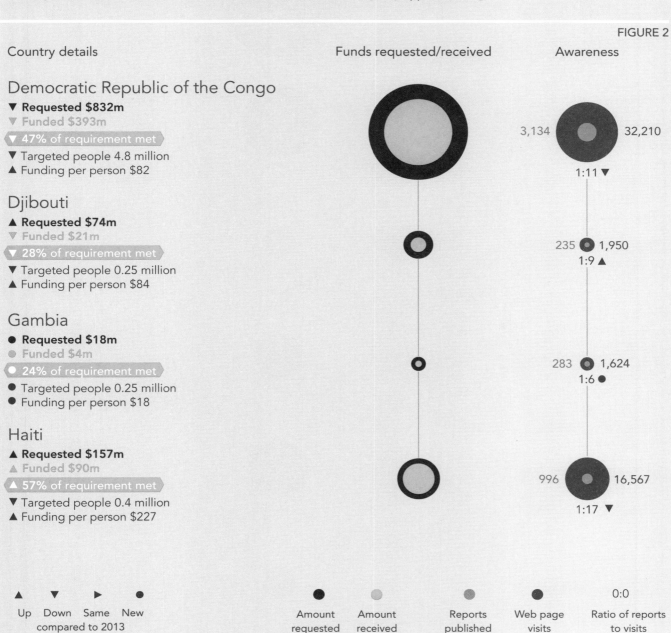

Country details — **Funds requested/received** — **Awareness**

Democratic Republic of the Congo
▼ **Requested $832m**
▼ Funded $393m
▼ 47% of requirement met
▼ Targeted people 4.8 million
▲ Funding per person $82

3,134   32,210
1:11 ▼

Djibouti
▲ **Requested $74m**
▼ Funded $21m
▼ 28% of requirement met
▼ Targeted people 0.25 million
▲ Funding per person $84

235   1,950
1:9 ▲

Gambia
● **Requested $18m**
● Funded $4m
● 24% of requirement met
● Targeted people 0.25 million
● Funding per person $18

283   1,624
1:6 ●

Haiti
▲ **Requested $157m**
▲ Funded $90m
▲ 57% of requirement met
▼ Targeted people 0.4 million
▲ Funding per person $227

996   16,567
1:17 ▼

▲ — ▼ — ▶ — ●
Up   Down Same New
compared to 2013

● Amount requested

● Amount received

● Reports published

● Web page visits

0:0
Ratio of reports to visits

Country details

Funds requested/received

Awareness

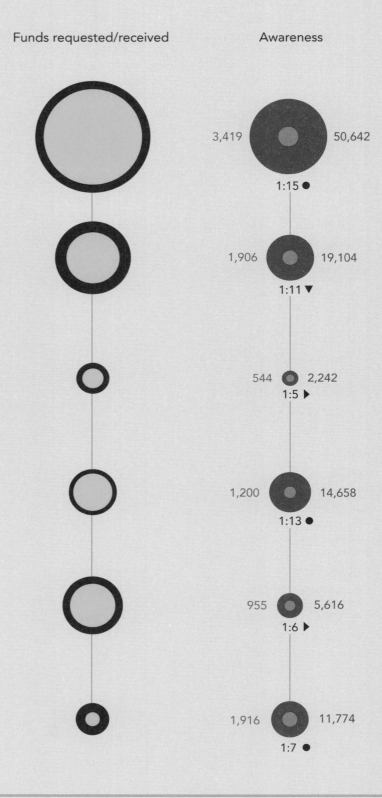

Iraq
- **Requested $1,113m**
- Funded $819m
- **74%** of requirement met
- Targeted people 1 million
- Funding per person $819

3,419   50,642

1:15 ●

Mali
- ▲ **Requested $481m**
- ▽ Funded $239m
- ▼ **50%** of requirement met
- ▼ Targeted people 1.6 million
- ▲ Funding per person $149

1,906   19,104

1:11 ▼

Mauritania
- ▼ **Requested $91m**
- ▽ Funded $38m
- ▼ **41%** of requirement met
- ▲ Targeted people 0.5 million
- ▼ Funding per person $71

544   2,242

1:5 ▶

Myanmar
- ● **Requested $192m**
- Funded $129m
- ○ **67%** of requirement met
- ● Targeted people 0.42 million
- ● Funding per person $306

1,200   14,658

1:13 ●

Niger
- ▼ **Requested $305m**
- ▽ Funded $173m
- ▼ **57%** of requirement met
- ▲ Targeted people 3.5 million
- ▼ Funding per person $49

955   5,616

1:6 ▶

Nigeria
- ● **Requested $93m**
- Funded $18m
- ○ **19%** of requirement met
- ● Targeted people 8.4 million
- ● Funding per person $2

1,916   11,774

1:7 ●

Sources: FTS, inter-agency appeal documents, ReliefWeb, UNHCR

Country details

Funds requested/received

Awareness

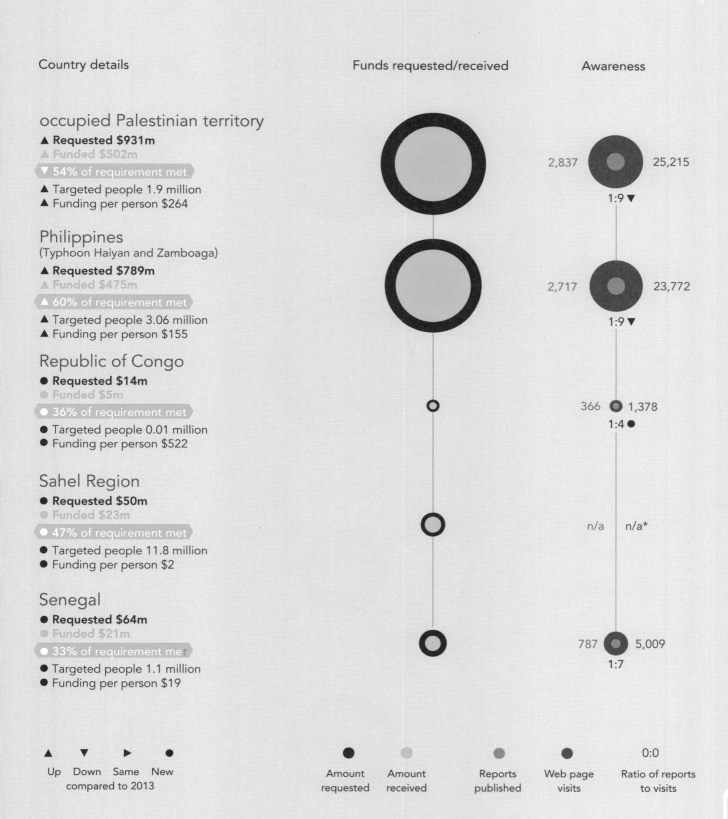

occupied Palestinian territory
▲ **Requested $931m**
△ Funded $502m
▼ 54% of requirement met
▲ Targeted people 1.9 million
▲ Funding per person $264

2,837　　　25,215

1:9 ▼

Philippines
(Typhoon Haiyan and Zamboaga)
▲ **Requested $789m**
△ Funded $475m
▲ 60% of requirement met
▲ Targeted people 3.06 million
▲ Funding per person $155

2,717　　　23,772

1:9 ▼

Republic of Congo
● **Requested $14m**
● Funded $5m
● 36% of requirement met
● Targeted people 0.01 million
● Funding per person $522

366 ● 1,378

1:4 ●

Sahel Region
● **Requested $50m**
● Funded $23m
● 47% of requirement met
● Targeted people 11.8 million
● Funding per person $2

n/a　　n/a*

Senegal
● **Requested $64m**
● Funded $21m
● 33% of requirement met
● Targeted people 1.1 million
● Funding per person $19

787 ● 5,009

1:7

▲　▼　▶　●

Up　Down　Same　New
compared to 2013

● Amount requested

● Amount received

● Reports published

● Web page visits

0:0
Ratio of reports to visits

Country details	Funds requested/received	Awareness

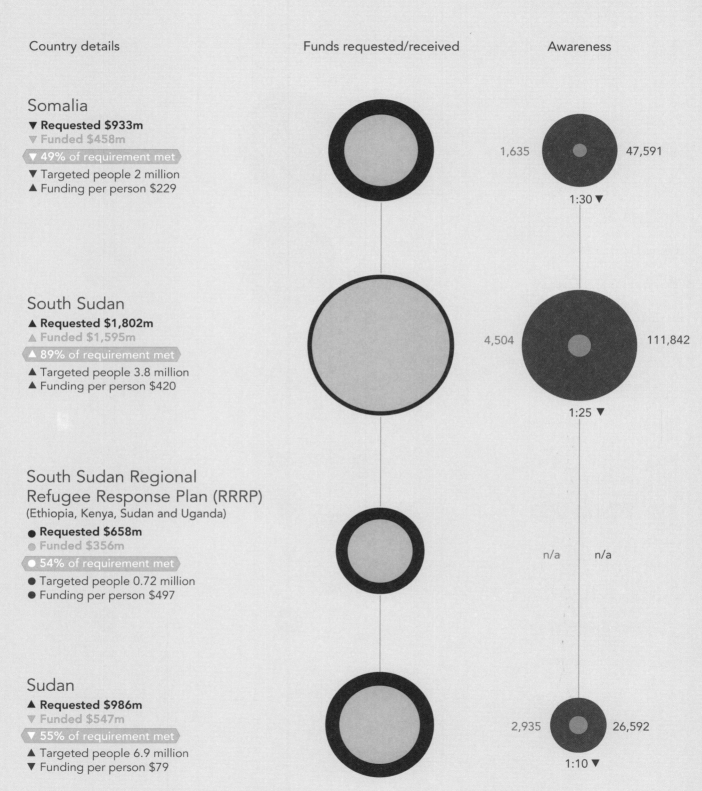

Somalia
▼ **Requested $933m**
▼ Funded $458m
▼ 49% of requirement met
▼ Targeted people 2 million
▲ Funding per person $229

1,635   47,591

1:30 ▼

South Sudan
▲ **Requested $1,802m**
▲ Funded $1,595m
▲ 89% of requirement met
▲ Targeted people 3.8 million
▲ Funding per person $420

4,504   111,842

1:25 ▼

South Sudan Regional Refugee Response Plan (RRRP)
(Ethiopia, Kenya, Sudan and Uganda)
● **Requested $658m**
● Funded $356m
● 54% of requirement met
● Targeted people 0.72 million
● Funding per person $497

n/a   n/a

Sudan
▲ **Requested $986m**
▼ Funded $547m
▼ 55% of requirement met
▲ Targeted people 6.9 million
▼ Funding per person $79

2,935   26,592

1:10 ▼

Sources: FTS, inter-agency appeal documents, ReliefWeb, UNHCR

Country details

Funds requested/received

Awareness

Syria Humanitarian Assistance Response Plan (SHARP)
▲ **Requested $2,256m**
△ Funded $1,123m
▼ 50% of requirement met
▲ Targeted people 10.8 million
▼ Funding per person $104

5,455

78,432

1:15 ▼

Syria Regional Response Plan (RRP)
▲ **Requested $3,741m**
△ Funded $2,333m
▲ 62% of requirement met
▲ Targeted people 6.6 million
▲ Funding per person $354

n/a

n/a

Yemen
▼ **Requested $596m**
▼ Funded $349m
▼ 59% of requirement met
▼ Targeted people 7.6 million
▼ Funding per person $46

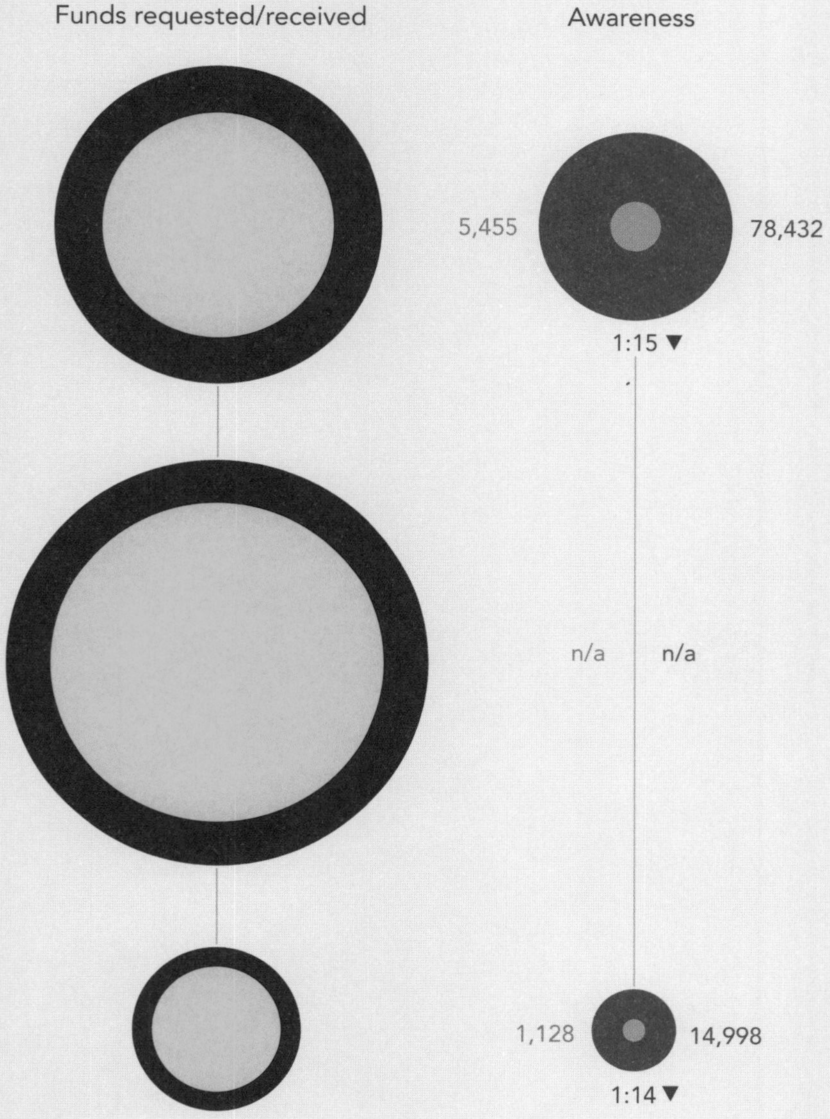

1,128

14,998

1:14 ▼

▲ ▼ ▶ ●
Up Down Same New
compared to 2013

● Amount requested

● Amount received

● Reports published

● Web page visits

0:0
Ratio of reports to visits

13

Humanitarian needs – sector funding

2014 saw a repeating pattern in terms of sector funding. Multisectoral programmes and the food-assistance sector continued to have the largest funding requests. Food assistance is generally the best-funded sector, but coordination and support services was the best-funded sector in 2014. It received a similar funding level in 2013 (77 per cent), so this change in pattern reflects decreasing funding levels for emergency food aid rather than increased support for coordination.

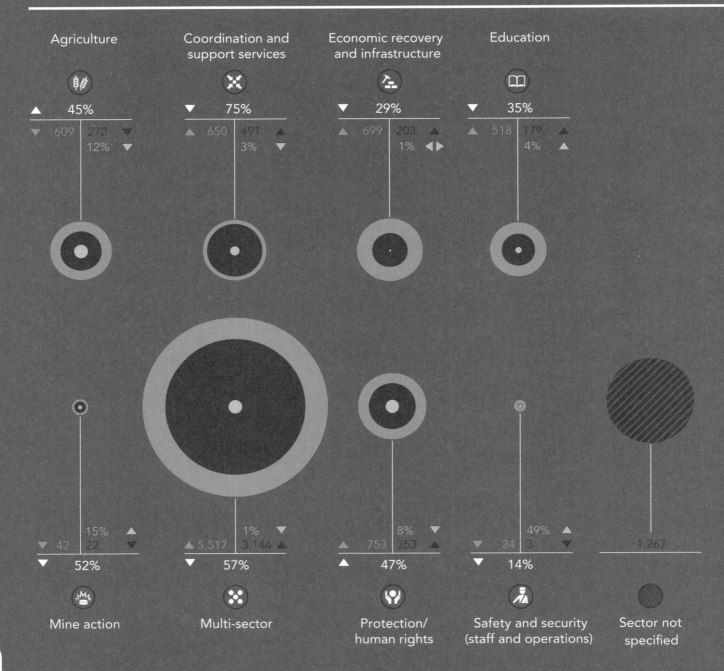

Agriculture	Coordination and support services	Economic recovery and infrastructure	Education
▲ 45%	▼ 75%	▼ 29%	▼ 35%
▼ 609 272 ▼	▲ 650 491 ▲	▲ 699 203 ▲	▲ 518 179 ▲
12% ▼	3% ▼	1% ◀▶	4% ▲

Mine action	Multi-sector	Protection/ human rights	Safety and security (staff and operations)	Sector not specified
15% ▲	1% ▼	8% ▼	49% ▲	
▼ 42 22 ▼	▲ 5,517 3,144 ▲	▲ 753 353 ▲	▼ 24 3 ▼	1,267
▼ 52%	▼ 57%	▲ 47%	▼ 14%	

Sources: CERF, inter-agency appeal documents, FTS

The Central Emergency Response Fund (CERF) comprised 4 per cent of the total funding available in 2014 ($412 million). This marked a slight decrease compared with 2013, when CERF contributed $482 million. Its largest contribution in absolute terms went to emergency food assistance ($109 million), and its largest contribution in percentage terms (49 per cent) went to one of the worst-funded sectors: safety and security of staff and operations. In 2014, only $6 million of CERF funding went towards projects addressing gender-based violence.

FIGURE 3

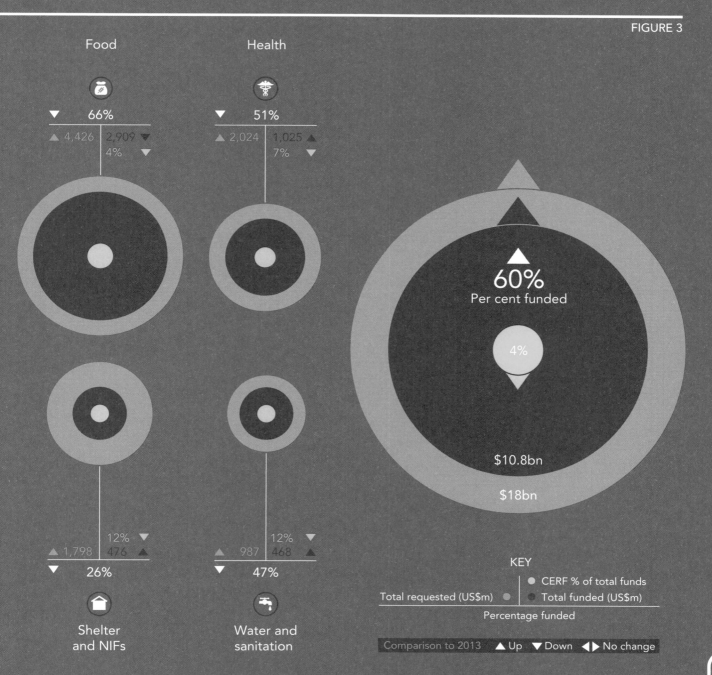

Food

▼ 66%
▲ 4,426 | 2,909 ▼
4% ▼

Health

▼ 51%
▲ 2,024 | 1,025 ▲
7% ▼

Shelter and NIFs

12% ▼
▲ 1,798 | 476 ▲
▼ 26%

Water and sanitation

12% ▼
▲ 987 | 468 ▲
▼ 47%

▲ 60%
Per cent funded
4%
$10.8bn
$18bn

KEY

● CERF % of total funds
Total requested (US$m) ● ● Total funded (US$m)
Percentage funded

Comparison to 2013   ▲ Up   ▼ Down   ◄► No change

Conflict in 2014

Forty-six extremely violent political conflicts took place in 2014, marking an increase of one compared to 2013. The total number of political conflicts increased by 10 to 424. The overall number of refugees and people forcibly displaced by violence or conflict increased by 8.3 million to reach a staggering 59.5 million people worldwide. The number of internally displaced persons (IDPs) increased by roughly 15 per cent to reach a new high of 38.2 million. There were

Number of people affected by conflict

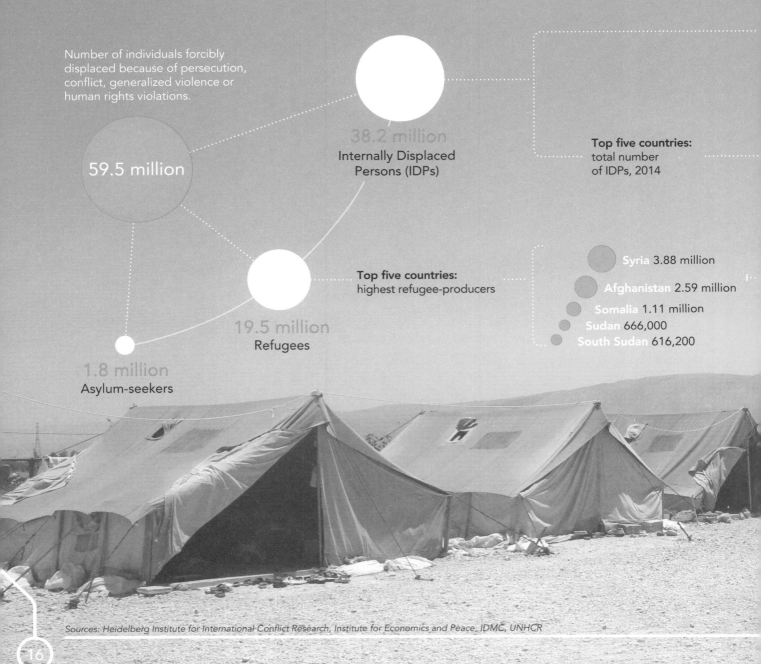

Number of individuals forcibly displaced because of persecution, conflict, generalized violence or human rights violations.

59.5 million

38.2 million
Internally Displaced Persons (IDPs)

Top five countries:
total number
of IDPs, 2014

Top five countries:
highest refugee-producers

Syria 3.88 million
Afghanistan 2.59 million
Somalia 1.11 million
Sudan 666,000
South Sudan 616,200

19.5 million
Refugees

1.8 million
Asylum-seekers

Sources: Heidelberg Institute for International Conflict Research, Institute for Economics and Peace, IDMC, UNHCR

approximately twice as many IDPs as refugees. Protracted crises in five countries—Democratic Republic of the Congo (DRC), Iraq, Nigeria, South Sudan and Syria—accounted for 60 per cent of new IDPs. In 2014, 51 per cent of refugees were under 18 years. The proportion of refugee girls and women has gradually increased from 48 per cent in 2011 to 50 per cent in 2014.

FIGURE 4

Top five countries:
number of new IDPs, 2014

Iraq 2.7 million
South Sudan 1.3 million
Syria 1.1 million
Democratric Republic of Congo 1 million
Nigeria 0.9 million

60%
new displacements

Syria 7.6 million
Colombia 6 million
Iraq 3.3 million
Democratic Republic of the Congo 2.7 million
Pakistan 1.9 million

56%
of the world's IDPs

45%
of the world's refugees

Number of conflicts*

Political conflicts	Violent crises	Highly violent crises
424	177	46

Economic cost of conflict
$14.3 trillion
equivalent to
13.4% of global GDP

17

Natural disasters in 2014

Roughly the same number of natural disasters occurred in 2014 as in 2013. However, the number of affected people increased from 97 million in 2013 to 141 million in 2014. This could be explained by an increase in the number of droughts. This was the only disaster category that registered an increase in 2014, and droughts accounted for 39 per cent of affected

Number of natural disasters	Number of countries affected	Number of affected people	Total damage
319	107	141 million	$110 billion

Top five countries by number of people affected

China
58 million ▶

Philippines
10 million ▶

India
5.7 million ▶

Burkina Faso
4 million ●

Sri Lanka
3 million ●

▶ Same   ● New – compared to 2013

Top five costliest disasters
US$ billions

7
Cyclone Hudhud
India

5
Drought
Brazil

5.9
Winter damage
Japan

5
Earthquake
China

5.1
Floods
India, Pakistan

Occurrence of disaster types

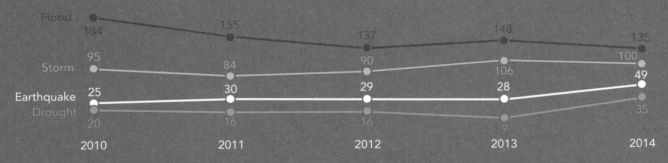

	2010	2011	2012	2013	2014
Flood	184	155	137	148	135
Storm	95	84	90	106	100
Earthquake	25	30	29	28	49
Drought	20	16	16	9	35

Sources: CRED EM-DAT, MunichRE

people. In terms of mortality, floods and landslides accounted for 63 per cent of fatalities. Forty-eight per cent of disasters occurred in Asia. Over 85 per cent of people killed and 86 per cent of those affected were also in Asia. As in 2013, China, the Philippines and India remained the top three countries in terms of the number of people affected.

FIGURE 5

Number of people affected by natural disaster per region

millions

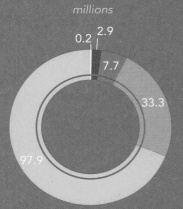

0.2   2.9
7.7
33.3
97.9

Numbers of disasters per region

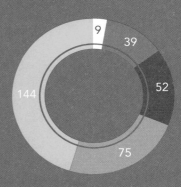

9
39
52
75
144

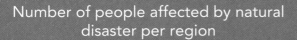

Oceania
Europe
Africa
Americas
Asia

Type of disasters per region

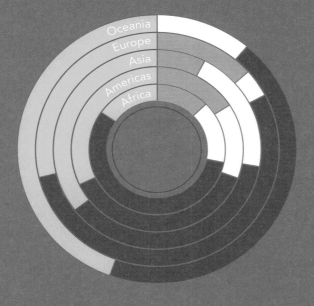

Oceania
Europe
Asia
Americas
Africa

● Drought   ● Earthquake   ● Flood   ● Storm

Global landscape

Conflicts and natural disasters have been seen as the main drivers of humanitarian need. They are often treated as discrete events, with little analysis of the underlying causes and warning signs. Today, the humanitarian landscape is changing more rapidly than ever. Global risks are recognized as increasingly central to humanitarian crises. They can make people more vulnerable and prevent them from building the resilience necessary to cope with shocks. The protracted and recurrent crises we see around the world today are a direct result of this vulnerability.

Food security

BASELINE: Of the world's 570 million farms, 9 out of 10 are run by families. Family farms produce about 80 per cent of the world's food. By 2014, approximately 805 million people were chronically undernourished, down more than 100 million over the last decade.

PROJECTION: In 2050, global food production will have to increase by 60 per cent from its 2005-2007 levels to meet increasing demand by the world's projected population of 9.7 billion.

Gender-based violence

BASELINE: One in every three women has been beaten, coerced into sex or abused in some other way, frequently by someone she knows. Globally, up to 38 per cent of murders of women are committed by an intimate partner. Six-hundred million women globally are living in countries where domestic violence is still not considered a crime.

PROJECTION: One in five women worldwide will become a victim of rape or attempted rape in her lifetime. The majority of these victims will be young women.

Pandemics

BASELINE: By the end of 2014, there were 12,861 confirmed cases of Ebola in Guinea, Liberia, and Sierra Leone. About 75 per cent of new human diseases are caused by microbes that originate in animals.

PROJECTION: Pandemics such as Ebola, MERS, HIV/AIDS and SARS will continue to be spurred by population growth, increased global trade and travel, global warming and poverty. Methods for dealing with pandemics will need to change from reactive to proactive to manage the threat.

Climate change

BASELINE: No year since 1880 has been as warm as 2014. In 2014, 48 per cent of disasters occurred in Asia. In East Asia and the Pacific, the number of people exposed to floods and tropical cyclones has increased by 70 per cent since 1980.

PROJECTION: Climate change may reduce raw water quality and pose risks to drinking water quality, even with conventional treatment. Climate change without adaptation will negatively affect crop production for local temperature increases of 2°C or more. Future annual losses due to disasters are estimated at $314 billion in built environments.

Diaspora

BASELINE: Remittances constitute the second largest source of foreign capital (after foreign direct investment). In 2014, 245 million migrants sent half a trillion dollars to their countries of origin, supporting on average 4.5 people each and affecting over 1 billion people worldwide.

PROJECTION: Diaspora groups are as diverse as the communities they serve, and there is not enough data to understand the capacities and role of the diaspora. In the humanitarian context, diaspora could become a key aid partner.

Economy

BASELINE: In 2014, global Gross Domestic Product (GDP) was $77.87 trillion, with an annual growth of 2.6 per cent. Inequality has reached unsurpassed levels: the richest 1 per cent of people own 48 per cent of global wealth. Of the remainder, 94.5 per cent is owned by the world's richest 20 per cent, leaving 5.5 per cent of global wealth to be distributed among 80 per cent of the world's population.

PROJECTION: Increasing inequality will result in the 1 per cent having more wealth than 99 per cent of the global population in the next two years. Global GDP is expected to increase to 3.1 per cent in 2016.

Sources: CRED, DESA, FAO, Global Slavery Index 2014, ILO, IOM, ITU, Millennium Development Goals Progress Report, NRC, Oxfam, UNHCR, UNISDR, UNDP, UNESCO, UNODC, UN Women, USAID, WHO, World Bank

In some cases, this vulnerability is exacerbated by the absence of a political solutions to conflicts. The humanitarian community has placed renewed emphasis on better understanding the drivers of crises, to move towards an evidence-based model where the root causes of humanitarian need are better understood and, therefore, the humanitarian community can serve affected people in a more effective way.

FIGURE 6

Health

BASELINE: Since 1990, the mortality rate for children under age 5 has declined by approximately 50 per cent. Maternal mortality has declined by 45 per cent. Pneumonia and diarrhoea account for 70 per cent of deaths in 15 countries, all of them in sub-Saharan Africa and Asia. Pneumonia kills 2,600 children a day.

PROJECTION: Unless early action is taken, preventable diseases will continue to be the main causes for the deaths of children under age 5.

Urbanization

BASELINE: In 2014, approximately 3.8 billion people lived in urban areas. Fifty-three per cent of the world's urban population lived in Asia, followed by Europe (14 per cent) and Latin America and the Caribbean (13 per cent).

PROJECTION: By 2050, 66 per cent of the world's population could live in urban areas, adding 2.5 billion people to urban populations. China, India and Nigeria are expected to account for 37 per cent of the world's urban population growth between 2014 and 2050.

Population

BASELINE: In 2014, the world's population was 7.2 billion people. Global population is increasing at a slower rate than 10 years ago, by 1.18 per cent annually, or 83 million people a year.

PROJECTION: By 2050, the world's population will increase to 9.7 billion people. More than half of the global increase will be in nine countries: DRC, Ethiopia, India, Indonesia, Nigeria, Pakistan, Tanzania, Uganda and the USA.

Migration

BASELINE: In 2014, over 22,000 migrants died en route to Europe. Of the 232 million global migrants, 72 million live in Europe. Youths aged between 15 and 24 account for approximately 12 per cent of international migrants.

PROJECTION: Family migration is the main and largest channel of entry for migrants, and it has great impact on human and economic development. Greater attention to coherent policy is necessary to assess the potential of the family unit in international migration, as well as protection challenges.

Technology

BASELINE: In 2014, there were 6.9 billion mobile telephone subscriptions. For every Internet user in the developed world, there are two in the developing world. However, two thirds of the population living in developing countries remain offline. Seventy-seven per cent of Twitter accounts were for users outside the United States.

PROJECTION: By the end of 2015, there will be 7 billion mobile telephone subscriptions, 5.5 billion of which will be from developing countries. There will be 3.2 billion Internet users, 2 billion of whom will be from developing countries.

Poverty

BASELINE: In 2014, an estimated 863 million people lived in slums, the majority in sub-Saharan Africa (approximately 200 million).

PROJECTION: By 2030, approximately 3 billion people will need adequate housing. To meet this, 96,150 housing units need to be completed per day from now until 2030.

 Increasing concern

 No change in concern

 Decreasing concern

Issues of increasing concern

Statelessness

BASELINE: A total of 3.5 million people are under UNHCR's statelessness mandate, but estimates indicate there are at least 10 million stateless people. Statelessness affects people in Asia and the Pacific more than the other regions. A total of 97.6 per cent of the number of reported stateless persons are found in 20 countries.

3.5 million
UNHCR statelessness mandate

found in 20 countries

PROJECTION: Statelessness destroys a person's political identity, leaving him/her more vulnerable to human rights violations. Statelessness can facilitate forced removal from a country. Statelessness may continue due to racial, ethnic or religious discrimination.

Children in conflict

BASELINE: In 2014, an estimated 230 million children lived in areas affected by armed conflicts. Nearly 15 million children were caught up in violent conflict in CAR, Iraq, Palestine, South Sudan, Syria and Ukraine.

PROJECTION: Children face tremendous challenges in conflict: hundreds are kidnapped going to/coming from school, tens of thousands are recruited or used by armed groups, and attacks on education and health facilities are increasing in many conflict areas.

Human trafficking

BASELINE: More than 90 per cent of countries have legislation criminalizing human trafficking. It is estimated that women account for 55 to 60 per cent of all trafficking victims detected globally. Women and girls together account for some 75 per cent, 27 per cent of victims are children.

Of all traffick victims detected globally

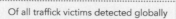

55-60%	75%	27%
Women	Women and girls	Children

PROJECTION: Despite legislative process to criminalize trafficking, there are few convictions for human trafficking.

Slavery and forced labour

BASELINE: Modern slavery comprises human trafficking, slavery/slavery-like practices (debt bondage, forced /servile marriage, sale/exploitation of children, descent-based slavery) and forced labour. An estimated 35.8 million men, women and children are in modern slavery globally. Sixty-one per cent of people are in five countries in Asia and Europe. Worldwide, approximately 14 per cent of girls aged between 5 and 14 are engaged in child labour, the majority unpaid.

35.8 million
people in modern slavery

in 5 countries

PROJECTION: The number of children recruited for child labour is decreasing, but the proportion of children in domestic work is increasing. Most countries provide some training to front-line law enforcement on how to identify victims of modern slavery, but victim assistance continues to be weak.

Sources: CRED, DESA, FAO, Global Slavery Index 2014, ILO, IOM, ITU, Millennium Development Goals Progress Report, NRC, Oxfam, UNHCR, UNISDR, UNDP, UNESCO, UNODC, UN Women, USAID, WHO, World Bank

 Increasing concern

200.5 million people were affected by natural disasters or displaced by conflict and violence.

Conflict and violence displaced 30,000 **people per day**.

Over 22,000 migrants **died** en route to Europe.

77 per cent of Twitter accounts were for users outside the United States.

Within the context of UN peace operations, humanitarian action was the costliest activity, **surpassing** the peacekeeping budget by $2 billion.

The **cost** of global conflict was estimated at $14.3 trillion.

19.3 million people were displaced by natural disasters; **91 per cent** of this displacement was due to weather-related events.

Civilians comprised 78 per cent of the almost 145,000 deaths and injuries caused by explosive weapons between 2011 and 2014.

Since 2006 85 per cent of CERF funding in Asia-Pacific has been used primarily to fund 5 sectors: food, WASH, health, shelter and logistics.

Between 2009 and 2014, the number of IDPs in the Middle East and North Africa region more than doubled from 6.7 million to 15.6 million.

Women accounted for 55 to 60 per cent of all human trafficking victims.

Only 4 per cent of projects in inter-agency appeals were gender-specific, showing no increase from previous years.

Key facts 2014

"To reaffirm humanity, we must also counteract the politicization of aid. In today's conflicts, life-saving assistance, like access to water or healthcare, is often used as a tool or a weapon ... All humanitarian action must seek not only to end suffering and meet immediate needs, but to keep people safe from harm and enable them to live with dignity."

Stephen O'Brien, **Emergency Relief Coordinator and Under-Secretary-General for Humanitarian Affairs, 2015**

REGIONAL
PERSPECTIVES

Responding to natural disasters in the Asia-Pacific region

Since the 2004 Indian Ocean tsunami, Governments in the Asia-Pacific region have increased their capacity to respond to natural disasters. Evidence for this can be seen in the increase in disaster management legislation passed, and the number of national disaster management authorities established in the past 10 years. These national disaster management authorities and systems are increasingly capable of managing an effective response to many of the disasters they face. Moreover, the growing prominence of bilateral response in the region and the intention of regional organizations to play a central role are changing the face of humanitarian response.

Asia-Pacific is the world's most disaster-prone region

88%

people affected by natural disasters world wide

40%

of global natural disasters

Between 2004 and 2014, the region accounted for...

53%

of the world's urban population

2 billion people
APPROXIMATELY
IN 2014

65%

of global economic losses

$162 billion

Average disaster losses per year

Changing the face of response

Over the last ten years, national authorities have taken considerable measures to invest in their response capacity to mitigate the effects of a disaster. They have done this, in part, through the establishment of national disaster management agencies.

Disaster Management Legislation (cumulative)

Number of National Disaster Management Authorities (cumulative)

2005	2006	2007	2008	2009	2010	2011	2012	2013	2014
12	14	21	23	24	26	27	29	30	31
12	14	16	18	19	22	23	24	26	26

Sources: CRED EM-DAT, OCHA ROAP

FIGURE 7

Areas at risk from earthquake activity and volcanic erruptions

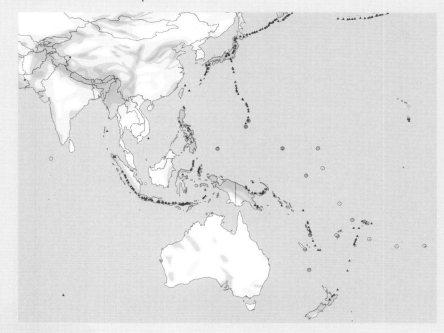

110

Number of earthquakes >Degree VII
2005-2014

The Asia-Pacific region encompasses both the Himalayan fault system and the Pacific Ring of Fire, making it one of the most seismically active regions in the world. Some of the most devastating earthquakes and tsunamis have occurred in this region. The map shows locations with a 20 per cent probability that the maximum degree of earthquake intensity will be exceeded in the next 50 years. Intensity is measured on a scale of one (feeble) to twelve (catastrophic).

Earthquake Intensity
Modified Mercalli Scale

- Degree I-V
- Degree VI
- Degree VII
- Degree VIII
- Degree IX-XII

Areas at risk from tropical storms

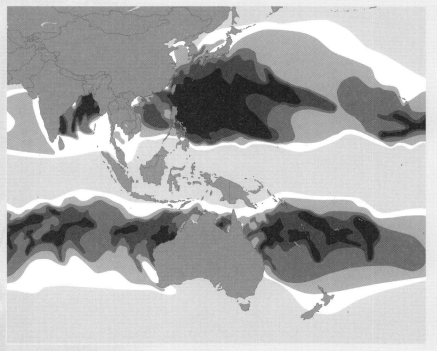

401

Number of tropical storms
2005-2014

There are three active storm basins in the Asia-Pacific region: the Northwest Pacific Basin, the South Pacific Basin and the Bay of Bengal. They have a combined average of 42 tropical cyclones per year. Some have resulted in catastrophic damage and losses and required a huge international humanitarian response. Nineteen of the 20 deadliest storms have occurred in the Asia-Pacific region. The map shows locations where there is a 10 per cent probability that storms of a given intensity will strike in the next 10 years.

Tropical Storm Intensity
Saffir-Simpson Scale

- One: 118-153 kmh
- Two: 154-177 kmh
- Three: 178-209 kmh
- Four: 210-249 kmh
- Five: 250+ kmh

Note: The boundaries and names shown and the desginations used on these maps do not imply official endorsement or acceptance by the United Nations

Initial response and key immediate needs

In many middle-income countries with substantial domestic capacity (see figure 7), the value of external assistance is increasingly seen as boosting the speed and volume of life-saving assistance provided in the early stages of the response, and augmenting national and regional capacity when affected States become overwhelmed. In the Asia-Pacific region, recent humanitarian operations have highlighted the need to realign international response in a way that supports communities, national and local authorities, and regional organizations. When humanitarian relief is delivered quickly and critical needs addressed immediately, communities are better placed to focus on restoring livelihoods and recovering from the shock.

Key immediate needs

Pre-identifying key immediate needs helps responders to be better prepared

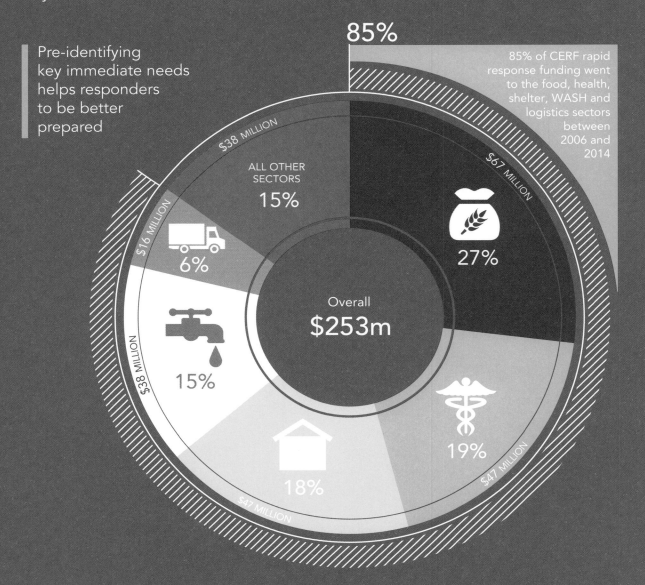

85%

85% of CERF rapid response funding went to the food, health, shelter, WASH and logistics sectors between 2006 and 2014

$38 MILLION

ALL OTHER SECTORS

15%

$16 MILLION

6%

$67 MILLION

27%

$38 MILLION

15%

Overall
$253m

18%

$47 MILLION

19%

$47 MILLION

Sources: CERF, OCHA ROAP

Several months into a response, the benefits of external assistance become less evident, as authorities regain their footing and become better positioned to manage recovery and reconstruction.

External assistance is most critical during the first one to three months of the response. Pre-identifying key immediate needs helps responders to be better prepared. A study of 31 CERF grants for rapid response in Haiti and the Asia-Pacific region showed that since 2006, nearly 85 per cent of CERF rapid-response funding has been used to support response in the food, health, shelter, WASH and logistics sectors. This is one example of how evidence-based planning can support a more effective humanitarian response.

FIGURE 8

Further analysis revealed that regardless of the disaster type, the key immediate needs remained the same.

Food   Health   Shelter/NFIs   WASH   Logistics   All other sectors

The impact of conflict on humanitarian action in the Middle East and North Africa region

The Middle East and North Africa region has witnessed an upsurge in violent conflict and displacement, particularly in the wake of the Arab revolutions. Since 2010, the number of conflicts, refugees and IDPs has grown in the region. Between 2009 and 2014, the number of conflicts increased by 35 per cent, from 55 to 74. In that same period, the number of IDPs more than doubled from 6.7 million to 15.6 million, while the number of refugees increased by nearly half from 5 million to 7.5 million. The upsurge in conflict has led to worrying patterns of sexual and gender-based violence targeting women, girls and minority groups. A convergence of factors related to culture, stigma and access to services all impact reporting, making it impossible to have an accurate picture of incidences, prevalence and dynamics.

Regional overview

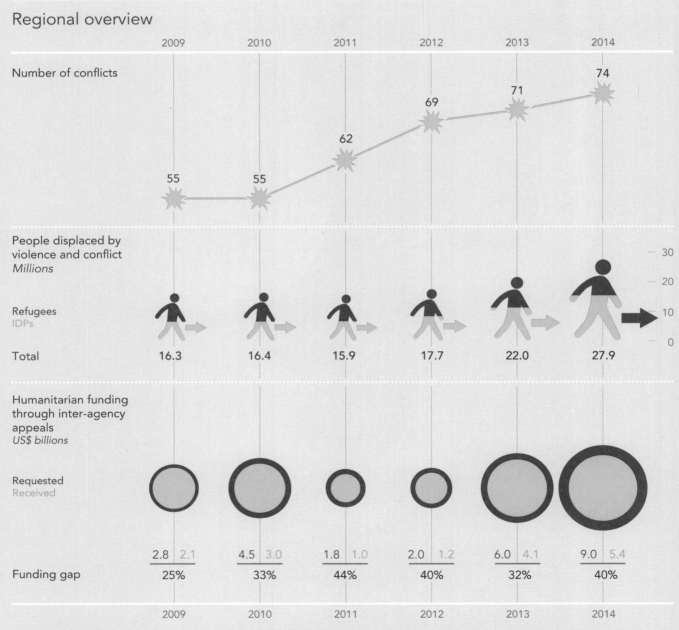

	2009	2010	2011	2012	2013	2014
Number of conflicts	55	55	62	69	71	74
People displaced by violence and conflict (Millions) — Total	16.3	16.4	15.9	17.7	22.0	27.9
Humanitarian funding through inter-agency appeals (US$ billions) Requested / Received	2.8 / 2.1	4.5 / 3.0	1.8 / 1.0	2.0 / 1.2	6.0 / 4.1	9.0 / 5.4
Funding gap	25%	33%	44%	40%	32%	40%

Sources: Aid Worker Security Database, Heidelberg Institute for International Conflict Research, IDMC, OCHA ROMENA, UNHCR, UNRWA

The humanitarian community has mobilized to provide life-saving assistance and protection to the most vulnerable people. The amount of funding requested through inter-agency appeals more than quadrupled between 2009 and 2014, while a record number of partner organizations participated in the appeals (373 in 2014) and contributed to the response. Humanitarian access and low funding levels continue to be challenges in aid delivery: on average, appeals in the region had a 36 per cent funding gap between 2009 and 2014, roughly the same as the global funding gap.

FIGURE 9

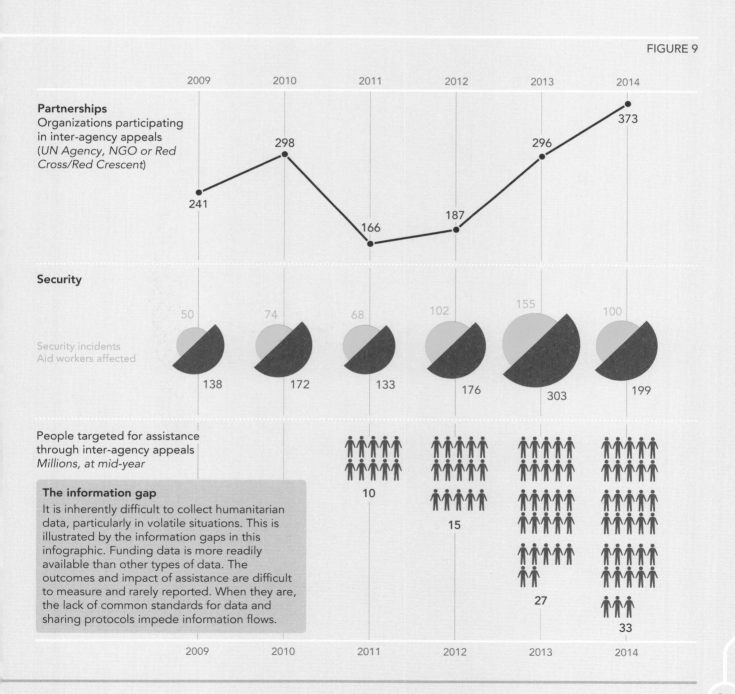

Partnerships
Organizations participating in inter-agency appeals (*UN Agency, NGO or Red Cross/Red Crescent*)

Security

Security incidents
Aid workers affected

People targeted for assistance through inter-agency appeals
Millions, at mid-year

The information gap
It is inherently difficult to collect humanitarian data, particularly in volatile situations. This is illustrated by the information gaps in this infographic. Funding data is more readily available than other types of data. The outcomes and impact of assistance are difficult to measure and rarely reported. When they are, the lack of common standards for data and sharing protocols impede information flows.

Afghanistan

"Despite more than a decade of international and government development efforts ... Afghanistan remains a protracted, complex emergency where five million people need life-saving assistance. This does not include the many more millions who are suffering the effects of chronic poverty." – Mark Bowden, Humanitarian Coordinator for Afghanistan, 2014

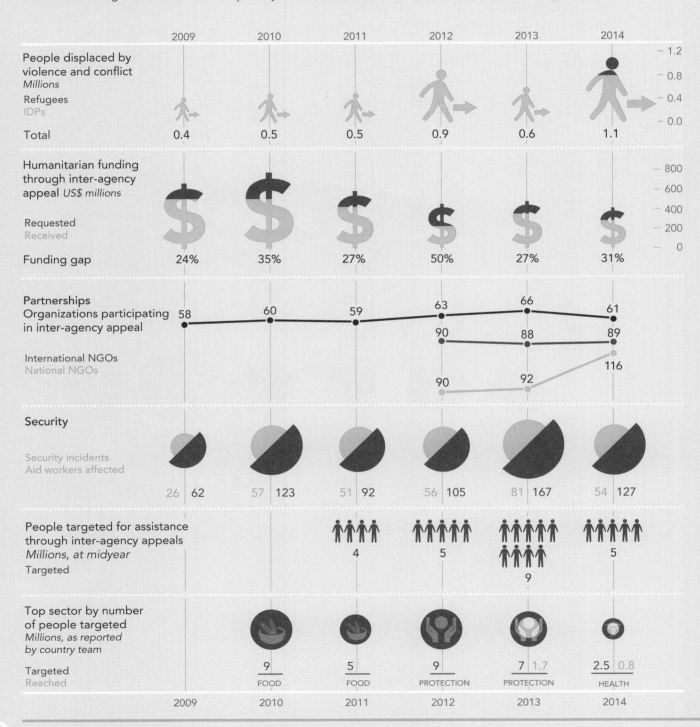

	2009	2010	2011	2012	2013	2014
People displaced by violence and conflict *Millions* Refugees IDPs						
Total	0.4	0.5	0.5	0.9	0.6	1.1
Humanitarian funding through inter-agency appeal *US$ millions* Requested Received						
Funding gap	24%	35%	27%	50%	27%	31%
Partnerships Organizations participating in inter-agency appeal	58	60	59	63	66	61
International NGOs				90	88	89
National NGOs				90	92	116
Security Security incidents Aid workers affected	26 / 62	57 / 123	51 / 92	56 / 105	81 / 167	54 / 127
People targeted for assistance through inter-agency appeals *Millions, at midyear* Targeted		4	5	9		5
Top sector by number of people targeted *Millions, as reported by country team* Targeted Reached		9 FOOD	5 FOOD	9 PROTECTION	7 / 1.7 PROTECTION	2.5 / 0.8 HEALTH

| | 2009 | 2010 | 2011 | 2012 | 2013 | 2014 |

Iraq

Since January 2014, 2.9 million people have fled their homes in three mass waves of displacement and multiple smaller ones. The humanitarian crisis in Iraq is a protection crisis above all else. Populations have been subjected to mass executions, systematic rape and horrendous acts of violence. Civilians who have remained in ISIL areas are at risk of reprisal by combatants as they retake territory from ISIL.

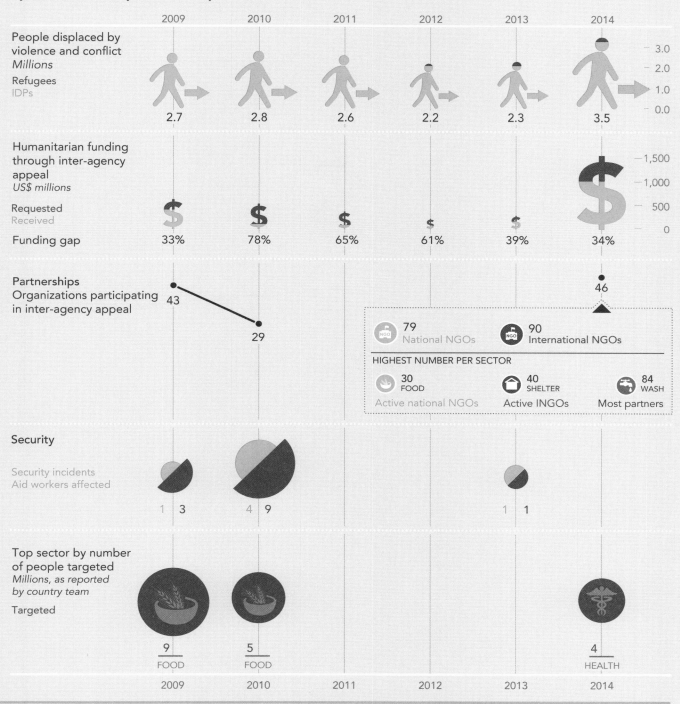

	2009	2010	2011	2012	2013	2014
People displaced by violence and conflict *Millions* — Refugees / IDPs	2.7	2.8	2.6	2.2	2.3	3.5
Humanitarian funding through inter-agency appeal *US$ millions* Requested / Received — Funding gap	33%	78%	65%	61%	39%	34%
Partnerships Organizations participating in inter-agency appeal	43	29				46

79 National NGOs
90 International NGOs

HIGHEST NUMBER PER SECTOR

30 FOOD	40 SHELTER	84 WASH
Active national NGOs	Active INGOs	Most partners

Security

Security incidents
Aid workers affected

2009	2010	2013
1 3	4 9	1 1

Top sector by number of people targeted
Millions, as reported by country team

Targeted

2009	2010	2014
9 FOOD	5 FOOD	4 HEALTH

2009	2010	2011	2012	2013	2014

Libya

Armed conflict and political instability have affected over 3 million people. Health and protection needs of the affected population stand out in terms of scope, scale and severity. The conflict has restricted access to basic services, led to forced displacement and impacted people's safety and security. Women, children, the elderly and those with low economic means are particularly vulnerable.

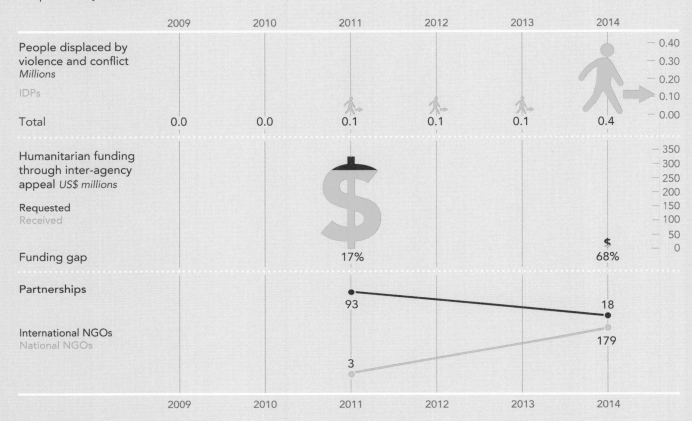

	2009	2010	2011	2012	2013	2014	
People displaced by violence and conflict *Millions*							— 0.40
							— 0.30
							— 0.20
IDPs							— 0.10
							— 0.00
Total	0.0	0.0	0.1	0.1	0.1	0.4	
Humanitarian funding through inter-agency appeal *US$ millions*							— 350
							— 300
							— 250
							— 200
Requested							— 150
Received							— 100
							— 50
Funding gap			17%			68%	— 0
Partnerships			93			18	
International NGOs							
National NGOs			3			179	

occupied Palestinian territory

"Since the conflict [in Gaza] began on 7 July 2014, at least 1,380 Palestinians civilians identified have been killed, including 423 children and 224 women, and over 9,000 people have been injured ... These recent impacts are all the more devastating as they take place against a backdrop of poverty, unemployment, food insecurity, and a failed economy – what many term the "de-development" of Gaza." - James W. Rawley, Humanitarian Coordinator oPt, 2014

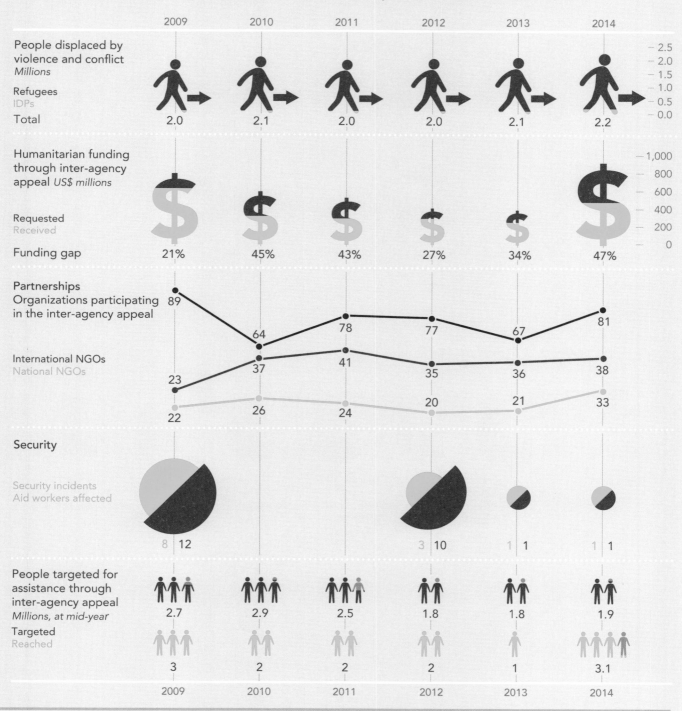

	2009	2010	2011	2012	2013	2014
People displaced by violence and conflict *Millions* — Refugees / IDPs / Total	2.0	2.1	2.0	2.0	2.1	2.2
Humanitarian funding through inter-agency appeal *US$ millions* — Requested / Received — Funding gap	21%	45%	43%	27%	34%	47%
Partnerships Organizations participating in the inter-agency appeal	89	64	78	77	67	81
International NGOs	23	37	41	35	36	38
National NGOs	22	26	24	20	21	33
Security — Security incidents / Aid workers affected	8 12			3 10	1 1	1 1
People targeted for assistance through inter-agency appeal *Millions, at mid-year* — Targeted	2.7	2.9	2.5	1.8	1.8	1.9
Reached	3	2	2	2	1	3.1

| 2009 | 2010 | 2011 | 2012 | 2013 | 2014 |

Pakistan

The displacement of population due to insecurity and natural disasters has been a major humanitarian concern for the past few years. Recurrent security operations in the north-west region displaced 1.6 million people in 2015. Monsoon floods in 2015 affected approximately 1.6 million people in more than 4,000 villages. Pakistan also suffers from a prevalence of under-nutrition with an estimated 14 million pregnant and lactating women and 22 million children affected.

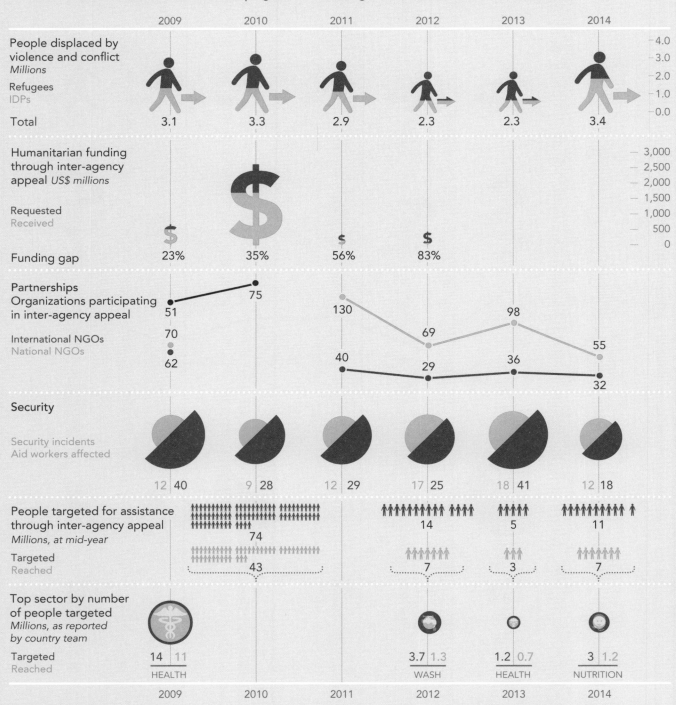

	2009	2010	2011	2012	2013	2014
People displaced by violence and conflict *Millions* Refugees IDPs						
Total	3.1	3.3	2.9	2.3	2.3	3.4
Humanitarian funding through inter-agency appeal *US$ millions* Requested Received						
Funding gap	23%	35%	56%	83%		
Partnerships Organizations participating in inter-agency appeal	51	75	130	69	98	55
International NGOs	70		40	29	36	32
National NGOs	62					
Security Security incidents Aid workers affected	12 40	9 28	12 29	17 25	18 41	12 18
People targeted for assistance through inter-agency appeal *Millions, at mid-year* Targeted	74			14	5	11
Reached	43			7	3	7
Top sector by number of people targeted *Millions, as reported by country team* Targeted Reached	14 11 HEALTH			3.7 1.3 WASH	1.2 0.7 HEALTH	3 1.2 NUTRITION

2009	2010	2011	2012	2013	2014

Syria

"In the past four years, the number of people in need of humanitarian assistance has increased twelve-fold. That figure is now 12.2 million. Nearly half of all Syrians have been forced from their homes: 7.6 million have been internally displaced and 3.9 million have fled to neighbouring countries, making this the largest displacement crisis in the world."
- Yacoub El Hillo, UN Resident and Humanitarian Coordinator for Syria, 2015.

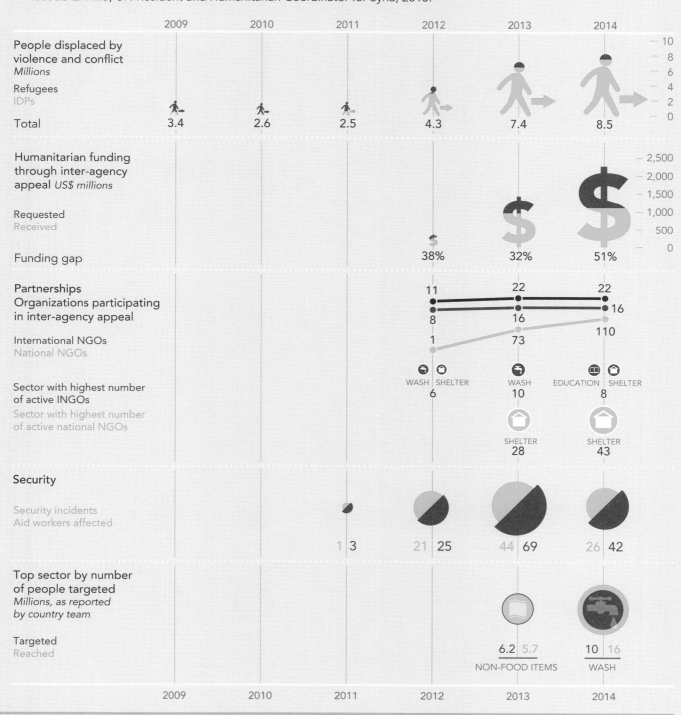

	2009	2010	2011	2012	2013	2014
People displaced by violence and conflict *Millions* / Refugees / IDPs — Total	3.4	2.6	2.5	4.3	7.4	8.5
Humanitarian funding through inter-agency appeal *US$ millions* Requested / Received — Funding gap				38%	32%	51%
Partnerships Organizations participating in inter-agency appeal International NGOs / National NGOs				11 / 8 / 1	22 / 16 / 73	22 / 16 / 110
Sector with highest number of active INGOs				WASH / SHELTER 6	WASH 10	EDUCATION / SHELTER 8
Sector with highest number of active national NGOs					SHELTER 28	SHELTER 43
Security Security incidents / Aid workers affected			1 | 3	21 | 25	44 | 69	26 | 42
Top sector by number of people targeted *Millions, as reported by country team* Targeted / Reached					6.2 | 5.7 NON-FOOD ITEMS	10 | 16 WASH

Scale for People displaced: 0, 2, 4, 6, 8, 10 (Millions)

Scale for Humanitarian funding: 0, 500, 1,000, 1,500, 2,000, 2,500

Yemen

Despite positive political developments in 2013, Yemen continues to be a large scale humanitarian crisis, with more than half the population or 14.7 million people in need of some form of humanitarian assistance.

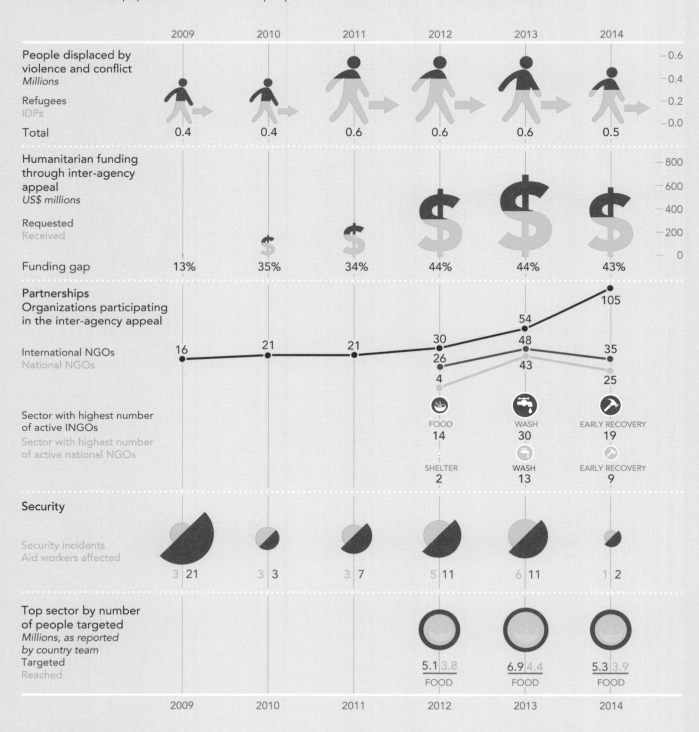

	2009	2010	2011	2012	2013	2014
People displaced by violence and conflict *Millions* Refugees IDPs						
Total	0.4	0.4	0.6	0.6	0.6	0.5
Humanitarian funding through inter-agency appeal *US$ millions* Requested Received						
Funding gap	13%	35%	34%	44%	44%	43%

Partnerships
Organizations participating in the inter-agency appeal

International NGOs
National NGOs

	2009	2010	2011	2012	2013	2014
	16	21	21	30	54	105
				26	48	35
				4	43	25

Sector with highest number of active INGOs

	2012	2013	2014
	FOOD	WASH	EARLY RECOVERY
	14	30	19

Sector with highest number of active national NGOs

	2012	2013	2014
	SHELTER	WASH	EARLY RECOVERY
	2	13	9

Security

Security incidents
Aid workers affected

	2009	2010	2011	2012	2013	2014
	3 | 21	3 | 3	3 | 7	5 | 11	6 | 11	1 | 2

Top sector by number of people targeted
Millions, as reported by country team
Targeted
Reached

	2012	2013	2014
	5.1 | 3.8	6.9 | 4.4	5.3 | 3.9
	FOOD	FOOD	FOOD

2009	2010	2011	2012	2013	2014

Regional refugee-hosting countries in focus

For decades, Jordan, Lebanon and Syria have been home to nearly half of all Palestinian refugees. Since 2013, the number of refugees in the region has increased drastically, particularly with Syrian refugees fleeing the conflict. The majority of refugees have fled to neighbouring countries, including Egypt, Jordan, Lebanon and Turkey. While some refugees are housed in camps, a vast proportion – approximately half – are living in urban areas, with different needs to refugees in camps.

The sheer scale of refugees in the region has opened up debate about how the international community can better support middle-income economies hosting large refugee populations, in particular, by making financing instruments accessible to them such as loans through international financial institutions. The scale of the refugee crisis has also renewed calls for supporting them in re-establishing a livelihood, to ultimately reduce vulnerability and need.

FIGURE 10

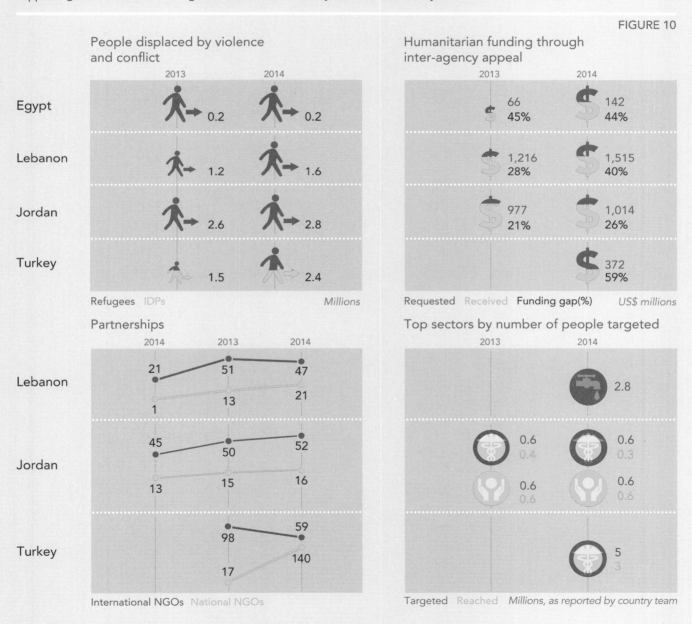

People displaced by violence and conflict

	2013	2014
Egypt	0.2	0.2
Lebanon	1.2	1.6
Jordan	2.6	2.8
Turkey	1.5	2.4

Refugees IDPs Millions

Humanitarian funding through inter-agency appeal

	2013	2014
Egypt	66 / 45%	142 / 44%
Lebanon	1,216 / 28%	1,515 / 40%
Jordan	977 / 21%	1,014 / 26%
Turkey		372 / 59%

Requested Received Funding gap(%) US$ millions

Partnerships

	2014	2013	2014
Lebanon	21 / 1	51 / 13	47 / 21
Jordan	45 / 13	50 / 15	52 / 16
Turkey		98 / 17	59 / 140

International NGOs National NGOs

Top sectors by number of people targeted

	2013	2014
Lebanon		2.8
Jordan	0.6 / 0.4 ; 0.6 / 0.6	0.6 / 0.3 ; 0.6 / 0.6
Turkey		5 / 3

Targeted Reached Millions, as reported by country team

Sources: Aid Worker Security Database, IDMC, OCHA ROMENA, UNHCR, UNRWA

"Technology and social media are giving people more access to more information than ever before. This connectivity means they can quickly reach out to others and form groups around issues. It has … empowered people in ways we would never have thought possible 25 years ago – and given them a much more powerful and audible voice to demand what they need."

Stephen O'Brien, **Emergency Relief Coordinator and Under-Secretary-General for Humanitarian Affairs, 2015**

TRENDS, CHALLENGES AND OPPORTUNITIES

The cost of humanitarian assistance

The humanitarian system has continued to professionalize and grow. Since 2004, the number of people targeted for assistance has more than doubled to reach 82.5 million in 2015, but the increase in funding requirements has risen at a much faster rate. In the same time frame, the cost of humanitarian assistance increased sixfold, from $3.4 billion to $19.5 billion. However, the number of inter-agency appeals has remained relatively stable at an average of 30 per year. Within the context of UN peace operations,* humanitarian action is the costliest activity. For example, in 2014, inter-agency appeal funding was more than $10 billion, while funding for peacekeeping operations stood at $8 billion.

Humanitarian funding through inter-agency appeals

US$ billions

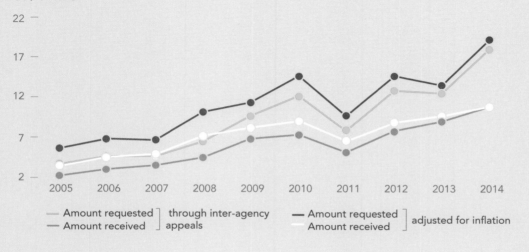

— Amount requested] through inter-agency
— Amount received] appeals

— Amount requested] adjusted for inflation
— Amount received]

Humanitarian action in the context of peace operations

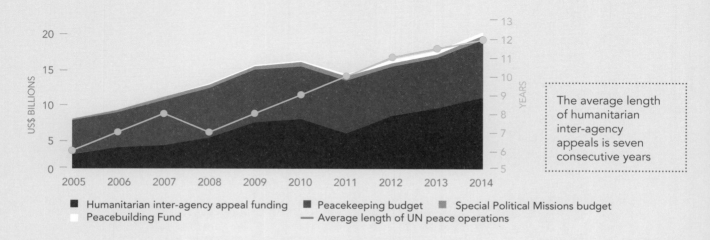

US$ BILLIONS

YEARS

■ Humanitarian inter-agency appeal funding   ■ Peacekeeping budget   ■ Special Political Missions budget
□ Peacebuilding Fund   — Average length of UN peace operations

> The average length of humanitarian inter-agency appeals is seven consecutive years

* Peace operations include peacekeeping operations, Special Political Missions and Peacebuilding Fund projects. Development activities are not included in this calculation (see technical note for more information). Sources: Aid Worker Security Database, FAO, FTS, OECD, UN University, UN budget documents, World Bank

Many factors play a role in explaining this cost increase, such as the complexity and length of crises, logistics and the upsurge in conflict. For example, funding for health and multisector projects (geared mostly towards IDPs and refugees) increased from $1.8 million in 2010 to $10.4 million in 2013. Surprisingly, inflation and drops in oil and food prices have not had as big an impact as envisaged. The fourfold increase in the number of appealing organizations since 2004, as well as the increase in funding per affected person (see figure 12), point to the most probable factor increasing the cost: the growth of projects per crisis as crises are prolonged and the layers of assistance increase.

FIGURE 11

People affected and people targeted for assistance

US$ millions

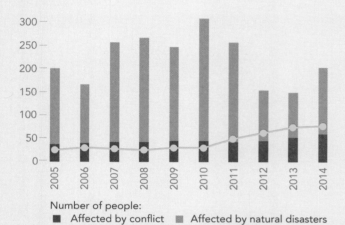

Number of people:
- ■ Affected by conflict
- ■ Affected by natural disasters
- Targeted through inter-agency appeals

Trends in energy, food and oil prices

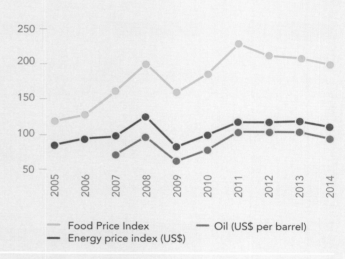

- Food Price Index
- Oil (US$ per barrel)
- Energy price index (US$)

Security for aid workers

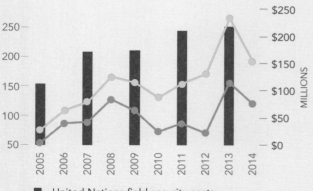

- ■ United Nations field security costs
- Number of security incidents against aid workers
- Number of aid workers killed

Number of projects and organizations participating in inter-agency appeals

US$ millions

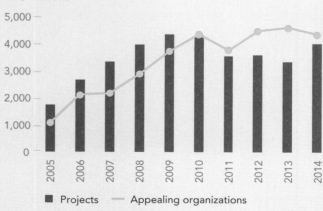

- ■ Projects
- Appealing organizations

43

The evolution of the Central Emergency Response Fund

CERF is one of the fastest and most effective ways to support rapid humanitarian response for people affected by natural disasters and armed conflict. The Fund, which is managed by the Emergency Relief Coordinator (ERC), has a $450 million annual funding target and receives voluntary contributions from donors year-round. This money is set aside for immediate use at the onset of emergencies, in rapidly deteriorating situations (rapid response) and in protracted crises that fail to attract sufficient resources (underfunded emergencies). CERF has a loan facility of up to $30 million

CERF was considered a bold innovation and one of the major successes of the 2005 humanitarian reform. As the global emergency response fund, it provides the ERC with a quick, flexible, impartial and reliable tool to support life-saving

CERF disbursements by year
US$ million

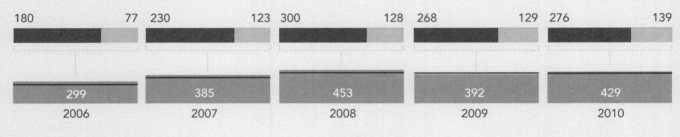

180	77	230	123	300	128	268	129	276	139
299		385		453		392		429	
2006		2007		2008		2009		2010	

Top 10 cumulative recipients of CERF funds, 2006 to 2014
US$ million

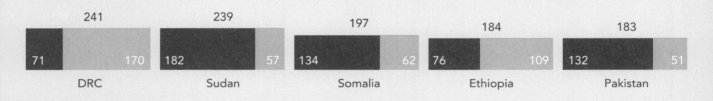

	241		239		197		184		183
71	170	182	57	134	62	76	109	132	51
DRC		Sudan		Somalia		Ethiopia		Pakistan	

Total CERF funding by sector, 2006 to 2014
US$ million

958	601	379	350	333	329	327
Food	Health	Water and sanitation	Shelter and non-food items	Multi-sector	Health – nutrition	Agriculture

Source: CERF

response worldwide. CERF allocates funds for life-saving activities on the basis of needs identified by humanitarian partners. CERF strengthens humanitarian response through reinforcing coordination, partnerships and leadership. Since its establishment, contributions to CERF have increased from $298 million in 2006 to $480 in 2014. CERF has disbursed approximately $421 million on average per year. Approximately two-thirds of CERF funds are allocated through the rapid response window and one third through the underfunded emergencies grants. To-date, CERF has supported life-saving humanitarian response in 94 countries and territories.

FIGURE 12

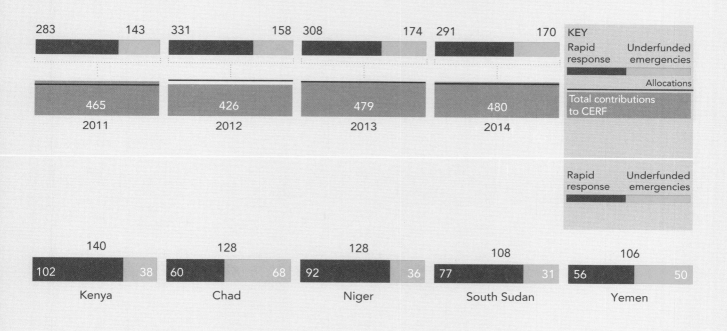

| 283 | 143 | 331 | 158 | 308 | 174 | 291 | 170 |

KEY

Rapid response — Underfunded emergencies

Allocations

Total contributions to CERF

| 465 | 426 | 479 | 480 |
| 2011 | 2012 | 2013 | 2014 |

Rapid response — Underfunded emergencies

140	128	128	108	106
102	38	60	68	92	36	77	31	56	50
Kenya	Chad	Niger	South Sudan	Yemen

| 188 | 159 | 51 | 14 | 12 | 11 |
| Coordination and stupport services | Protection/Human Rights/Rule of Law | Education | Economic recovery and infrastructure | Security | Mine action |

The evolution of country-based pooled funds

Country-based pooled funds (CBPFs) are multi-donor humanitarian financing instruments established by the Emergency Relief Coordinator (ERC). These innovative humanitarian funds allow governments and private donors alike to pool their contributions to support a specific emergency. CBPFs are managed by OCHA at the country-level under the leadership of the Humanitarian Coordinator (HC). They complement other sources of funding, are field-driven and aligned with country humanitarian response plans (HRPs). This ensures that flexible, coordinated, inclusive and needs-based funding is available and prioritized at the local level by the relief partners closest to people in need.

Common Humanitarian Funds

US$ millions

CHF funding by country

5.	Central African Republic	Central African Republic	Central African Republic	Central African Republic
4. Central African Republic	4. S. Sudan	4. Somalia	4. Somalia	4. Somalia
3. Somalia	3. DRC	3. Sudan	3. Sudan	3. Sudan
2. Sudan	2. Sudan	2. DRC	2. DRC	2. DRC
1. DRC	1. Somalia	1. S. Sudan	1. S. Sudan	1. S. Sudan

CHF funding per year

215	348	364	334	321
2010	2011	2012	2013	2014

CHF allocations by sector

1. Health	1. Health	1. Health	1. Health	1. Health
2. Water	2. Water	2. Water	2. Support	2. Water
3. Shelter	3. Agriculture	3. Agriculture	3. Water	3. Support
4. Agriculture	4. Support	4. Support	4. Agriculture	4. Shelter
5. Support	5. Shelter	5. Food	5. Not specified	5. Food

Sources: FTS, OCHA

Donor contributions to each CBPF are un-earmarked and allocated by the HC through an in-country consultative process. They provide rapid funding to scale up humanitarian operations, fill critical gaps and strengthen partnerships with aid organizations, including local and international NGOs. OCHA currently manages pooled funds in 18 countries and ensures the systemized use of the gender marker in funding decisions. CBPFs have received more than $2.2 billion in contributions since 2011. Until 2014, there were two types of CBPFs: Common Humanitarian Funds and Emergency Respoonse Funds. Since 2015, the distinction is no longer in use.

Emergency Response Funds

US$ millions

FIGURE 13

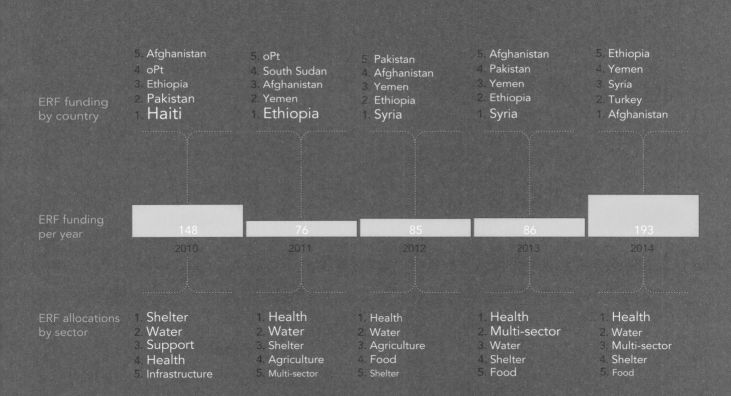

ERF funding by country

2010	2011	2012	2013	2014
5. Afghanistan	5. oPt	5. Pakistan	5. Afghanistan	5. Ethiopia
4. oPt	4. South Sudan	4. Afghanistan	4. Pakistan	4. Yemen
3. Ethiopia	3. Afghanistan	3. Yemen	3. Yemen	3. Syria
2. Pakistan	2. Yemen	2. Ethiopia	2. Ethiopia	2. Turkey
1. Haiti	1. Ethiopia	1. Syria	1. Syria	1. Afghanistan

ERF funding per year

2010	2011	2012	2013	2014
148	76	85	86	193

ERF allocations by sector

2010	2011	2012	2013	2014
1. Shelter	1. Health	1. Health	1. Health	1. Health
2. Water	2. Water	2. Water	2. Multi-sector	2. Water
3. Support	3. Shelter	3. Agriculture	3. Water	3. Multi-sector
4. Health	4. Agriculture	4. Food	4. Shelter	4. Shelter
5. Infrastructure	5. Multi-sector	5. Shelter	5. Food	5. Food

Until 2014, there were two types of CBPFs: Common Humanitarian Funds (CHFs) and Emergency Response Funds (ERFs). CHFs were used normally for projects in a Strategic Response Plan for large, persistent emergencies. ERFs were mostly used to address unforeseen humanitarian needs. Between 2010 and 2014, the health sector received the most funding from both CHFs and ERFs. On average, 14 countries have received an ERF per year and five countries have received a CHF. With the issuance of the global guidelines on CBPFs in 2015, OCHA is moving away from the distinction between CHFs and ERFs in an effort to streamline the funds' management and operation. All CBPFs will be primarily aligned to support the delivery of the Humanitarian Response Plans (HRPs), while retaining the flexibility to allocate funds to unforeseen events.

Funding trends: where does the money come from?

Humanitarian spending is usually a very small portion of financial support provided to a country. Humanitarian funding is a small proportion of overall Official Development Assistance (ODA), and it pales in comparison to development funding, remittances and foreign direct investment. Donor governments, particularly OECD-DAC Member States, tend to provide the largest contributions to humanitarian assistance, but other donors and private organizations are increasing their support. A study of a complex crisis (Iraq) and a natural disaster (Philippines) showed that funding patterns were strikingly similar, with humanitarian assistance being only a small portion of ODA, overshadowed by remittances and/or foreign direct investment.

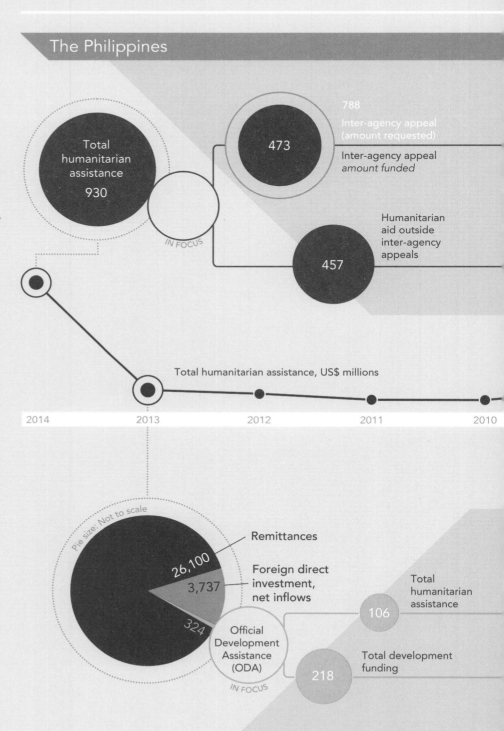

The Philippines

Total humanitarian assistance
930

473

788
Inter-agency appeal
(amount requested)

Inter-agency appeal
amount funded

Humanitarian aid outside inter-agency appeals
457

IN FOCUS

Total humanitarian assistance, US$ millions

2014   2013   2012   2011   2010

Pie size: Not to scale

Remittances
26,100

Foreign direct investment, net inflows
3,737

324

Official Development Assistance (ODA)

IN FOCUS

Total humanitarian assistance
106

Total development funding
218

Sources: FTS, OCHA, OECD, World Bank

FIGURE 14

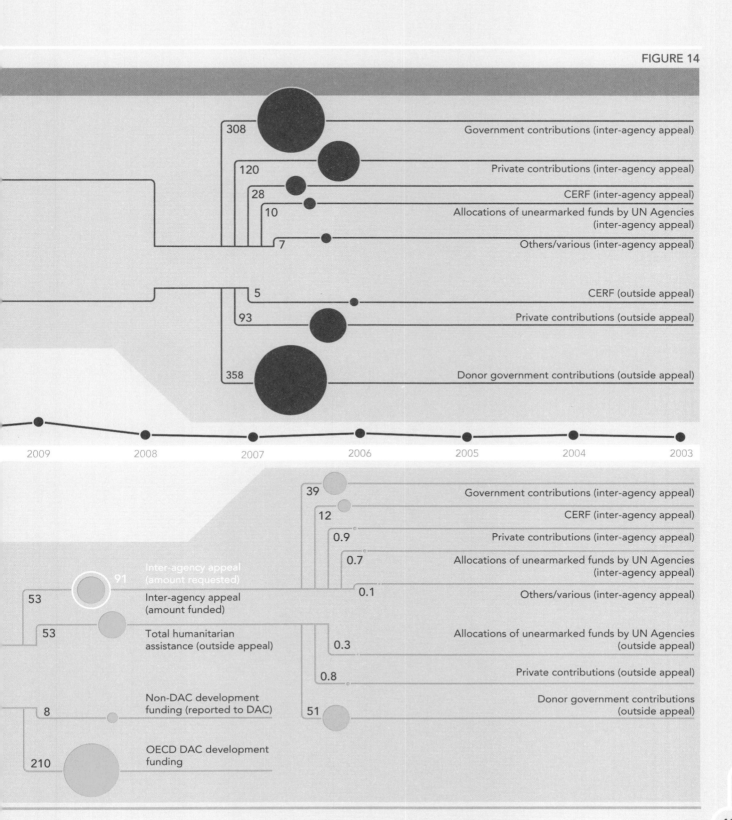

308 — Government contributions (inter-agency appeal)

120 — Private contributions (inter-agency appeal)

28 — CERF (inter-agency appeal)

10 — Allocations of unearmarked funds by UN Agencies (inter-agency appeal)

7 — Others/various (inter-agency appeal)

5 — CERF (outside appeal)

93 — Private contributions (outside appeal)

358 — Donor government contributions (outside appeal)

2009   2008   2007   2006   2005   2004   2003

39 — Government contributions (inter-agency appeal)

12 — CERF (inter-agency appeal)

0.9 — Private contributions (inter-agency appeal)

0.7 — Allocations of unearmarked funds by UN Agencies (inter-agency appeal)

91 — Inter-agency appeal (amount requested)

53 — Inter-agency appeal (amount funded)

0.1 — Others/various (inter-agency appeal)

53 — Total humanitarian assistance (outside appeal)

0.3 — Allocations of unearmarked funds by UN Agencies (outside appeal)

0.8 — Private contributions (outside appeal)

8 — Non-DAC development funding (reported to DAC)

51 — Donor government contributions (outside appeal)

210 — OECD DAC development funding

In the cases of Iraq and the Philippines, humanitarian funding was small compared to ODA. 2013 is the last year for which full financial data is available. In that year, humanitarian assistance was 15 per cent of overall ODA. In turn, overall ODA was only half the size of foreign direct investment. The largest donor region for Iraq was the Middle East.

In the Philippines in 2013, humanitarian assistance was 32 per cent of overall ODA. Remittances, however, were nearly 80 times the amount of ODA. At a time when the cost of humanitarian assistance is increasing, humanitarian responders must look to other funding sources to continue to meet the needs of affected people.

Iraq

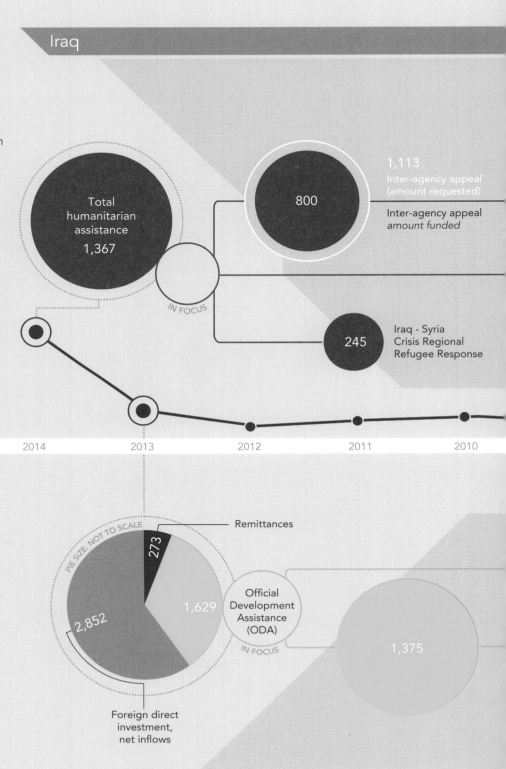

Total humanitarian assistance
1,367

1,113
Inter-agency appeal (amount requested)

Inter-agency appeal *amount funded*

800

IN FOCUS

245
Iraq - Syria Crisis Regional Refugee Response

2014   2013   2012   2011   2010

PIE SIZE: NOT TO SCALE

Remittances

273

1,629

Official Development Assistance (ODA)

IN FOCUS

2,852

1,375

Foreign direct investment, net inflows

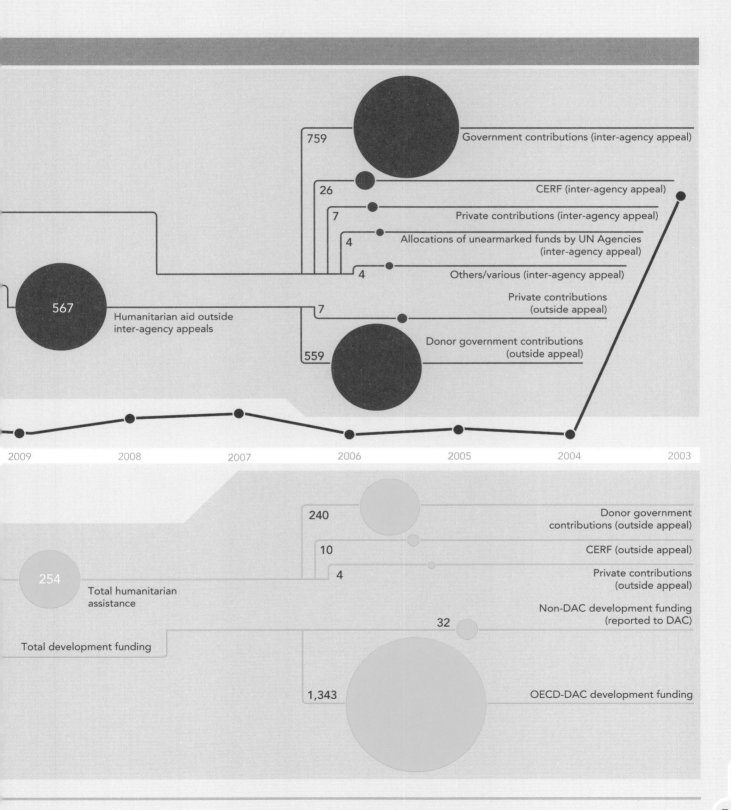

759 — Government contributions (inter-agency appeal)

26 — CERF (inter-agency appeal)

7 — Private contributions (inter-agency appeal)

4 — Allocations of unearmarked funds by UN Agencies (inter-agency appeal)

4 — Others/various (inter-agency appeal)

7 — Private contributions (outside appeal)

559 — Donor government contributions (outside appeal)

567 — Humanitarian aid outside inter-agency appeals

2009 2008 2007 2006 2005 2004 2003

240 — Donor government contributions (outside appeal)

10 — CERF (outside appeal)

4 — Private contributions (outside appeal)

Non-DAC development funding (reported to DAC)

32

254 — Total humanitarian assistance

Total development funding

1,343 — OECD-DAC development funding

The humanitarian-development nexus in protracted crises

To date, there have been six crises with an inter-agency appeal renewed for ten consecutive years or more: Chad, Central African Republic (CAR), Democratic Republic of Congo (DRC), occupied Palestinian territory (oPt), Somalia and Sudan. Beyond their protracted nature, these crises exhibit links between development indicators and humanitarian action in-country. Over the last five years, as funding per person has increased, development indicators have improved. In some cases, the cause of the increase in per capita spending was directly related to a major emergency, such as the 2013 conflict in CAR. But this is not necessarily the case in all instances.

Funding per targeted person
US$

	2011	2012	2013	2014
DRC	$65	$113	$161	$80
CAR	$40	$40	$171	$219
Chad	$125	$198	$165	$119
oPt	$95	$76	$70	$248
Somalia	$191	$298	$145	$260
Sudan	$75	$146	$136	$77
Average	$99	$145	$141	$167

Sources: FTS, World Justice Project - Rule of Law Index, UNDP, World Bank

The success of the Millennium Development Goals has contributed to improvement of development, but the expansion of humanitarian action may also be playing a role in promoting development. Humanitarian and development action share a goal to build local capacities and improve resilience, but there is a question about the extent to which humanitarians have become involved in development work. The most important question is how humanitarians and development actors can build more effective partnerships to make better use of scarce resources.

Select development indicators

FIGURE 15

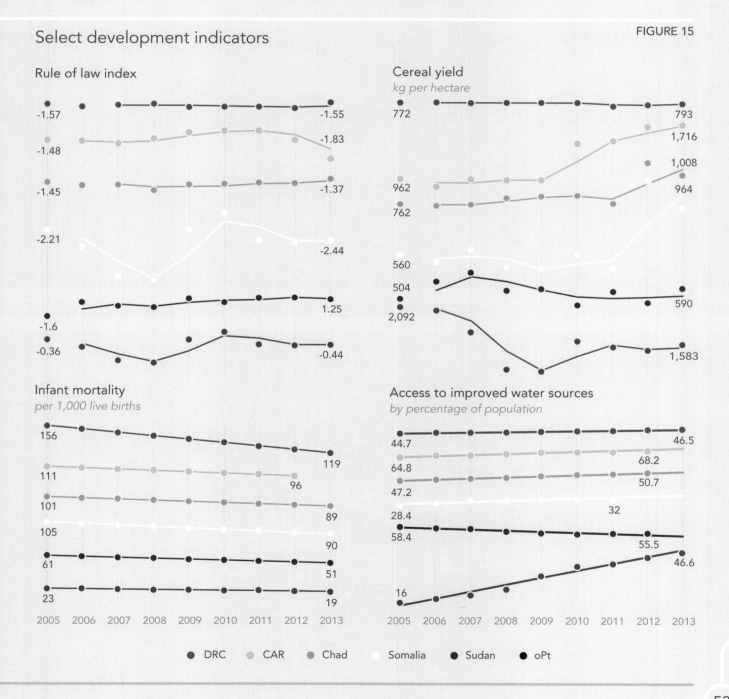

Rule of law index

-1.57   -1.55
-1.48   -1.83
-1.45   -1.37
-2.21   -2.44
    1.25
-1.6
-0.36   -0.44

Cereal yield
kg per hectare

772   793
    1,716
    1,008
962   964
762
560
504
    590
2,092
    1,583

Infant mortality
per 1,000 live births

156   119
111   96
101   89
105   90
61   51
23   19

2005 2006 2007 2008 2009 2010 2011 2012 2013

Access to improved water sources
by percentage of population

44.7   46.5
64.8   68.2
47.2   50.7
28.4   32
58.4   55.5
    46.6
16

2005 2006 2007 2008 2009 2010 2011 2012 2013

● DRC   ● CAR   ● Chad   ○ Somalia   ● Sudan   ● oPt

Measuring impact: the case of Darfur

The protracted humanitarian crisis in Darfur has required annual inter-agency humanitarian appeals since the conflict began in 2003. But despite the presence of peacekeepers, aid workers and development actors, there has been no significant improvement in the region's development. Insecurity and instability have continued to generate humanitarian needs, and 2014 saw the highest level of new displacement for a decade. The operating environment for aid organizations remains extremely challenging. While the majority of people in need can be reached, some areas have not been accessed for several years.

Dafur: timeline of events

 989,920

853,000

February 2003	April 2003	January 2004	April 2004
Armed movements in Darfur begin attacking government installations. They claim the Sudanese Government is neglecting the region.	Armed movements attack Sudanese Armed Forces (SAF) at El Fasher Airport. This is the first direct attack in a major town.	SAF begins a military campaign to stop the armed movements in Darfur's western region. Hundreds of thousands of people are internally displaced or flee to Chad.	On April 8, the Humanitarian Ceasefire Agreeement is signed. This agreement committed the Sudanese Government to facilitating humanitarian assistance.

2003   2004

2016   2015   2014

July 2015	January 2015	December 2014	May 2014
Humanitarian partners verify more than 80,000 new IDPs, but are unable to confirm reports of close to 100,000 other newly displaced people due to access constraints.	Operations against armed movements continue to cause displacement of civilians in North Darfur and around Jebel Marra. Jebel Marra remains largely inaccessible to humanitarian organizations.	The Government announces a second phase of "Operation Decisive Summer".	The Government announces "Operation Decisive Summer" to end rebellion in Darfur, South Kordofan and Blue Nile. The operation involves deploying Rapid Support Forces which were allegedly involved in attacks against civilians in South Darfur in February 2014.

KEY

 Peacekeepers (UNAMID)

 International NGOs

 Aid workers

 IDPs

Inter-tribal fighting, operations against armed movements and attacks by armed movements displace an estimated 430,000 people - the highest level of displacement since 2003.

 19,248

 5,540

 430,000

Sources: FTS, Feinstein International Center, FTS, International Peace Institute, OCHA Sudan, ReliefWeb, UNDP, World Bank

Funding shortfalls have been growing steadily, with just 55 per cent of requirements covered in 2014. Analysis of the ratio of ReliefWeb reports on Sudan compared to web page visits suggests a decline in public attention: interest in the crisis has waned since 2008 with fewer web page visits, despite an increase in the number of reports produced on Darfur.

FIGURE 16

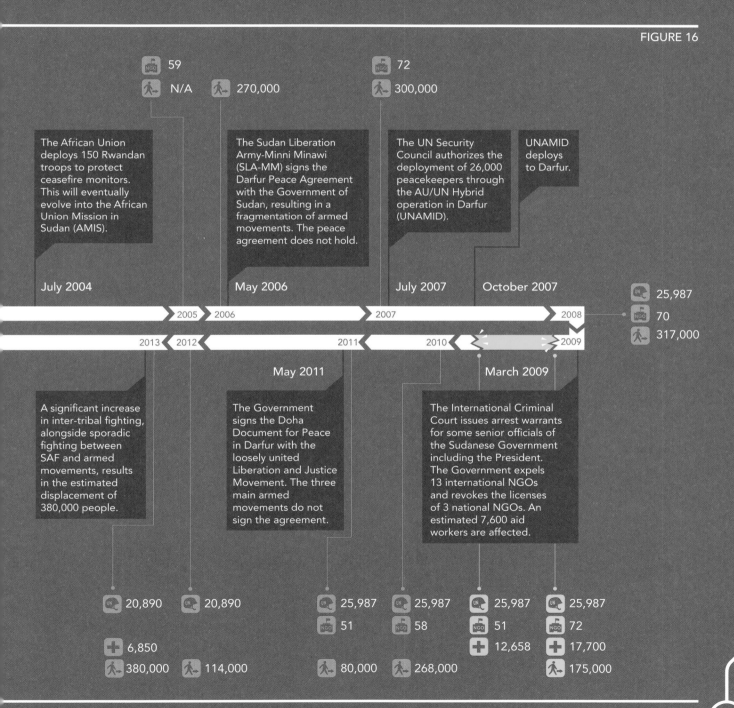

NGO 59
🚶 N/A

🚶 270,000

NGO 72
🚶 300,000

The African Union deploys 150 Rwandan troops to protect ceasefire monitors. This will eventually evolve into the African Union Mission in Sudan (AMIS).

July 2004

The Sudan Liberation Army-Minni Minawi (SLA-MM) signs the Darfur Peace Agreement with the Government of Sudan, resulting in a fragmentation of armed movements. The peace agreement does not hold.

May 2006

The UN Security Council authorizes the deployment of 26,000 peacekeepers through the AU/UN Hybrid operation in Darfur (UNAMID).

July 2007

UNAMID deploys to Darfur.

October 2007

2005 2006 2007 2008

UN 25,987
NGO 70
🚶 317,000

2013 2012 2011 2010 2009

May 2011

March 2009

A significant increase in inter-tribal fighting, alongside sporadic fighting between SAF and armed movements, results in the estimated displacement of 380,000 people.

The Government signs the Doha Document for Peace in Darfur with the loosely united Liberation and Justice Movement. The three main armed movements do not sign the agreement.

The International Criminal Court issues arrest warrants for some senior officials of the Sudanese Government including the President. The Government expels 13 international NGOs and revokes the licenses of 3 national NGOs. An estimated 7,600 aid workers are affected.

UN 20,890

UN 20,890

UN 25,987
NGO 51

UN 25,987
NGO 58

UN 25,987
NGO 51
➕ 12,658

UN 25,987
NGO 72
➕ 17,700

➕ 6,850
🚶 380,000

🚶 114,000

🚶 80,000

🚶 268,000

🚶 175,000

Development indicators for Sudan

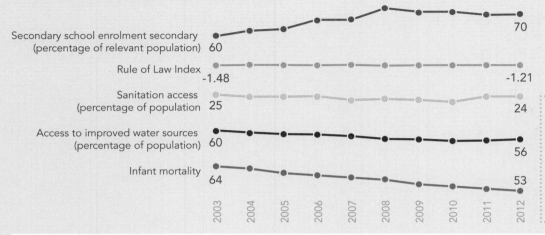

Secondary school enrolment secondary
(percentage of relevant population) 60 — 70

Rule of Law Index
-1.48 — -1.21

Sanitation access
(percentage of population 25 — 24

Access to improved water sources
(percentage of population) 60 — 56

Infant mortality
64 — 53

2003 2004 2005 2006 2007 2008 2009 2010 2011 2012

Between 2008 and 2012, the **Human Development Index** for Sudan has increased marginally from 0.447 to 0.472. In 2013, it was ranked 166 out of 187 countries in terms of human development.

Financial indicators

US$ billions

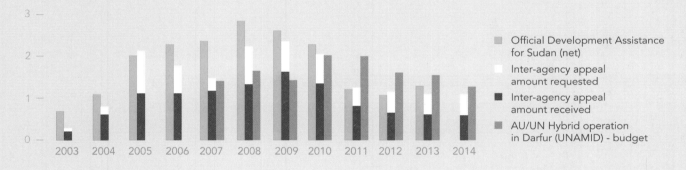

3 —

2 —

1 —

0 —

2003 2004 2005 2006 2007 2008 2009 2010 2011 2012 2013 2014

■ Official Development Assistance for Sudan (net)

□ Inter-agency appeal amount requested

■ Inter-agency appeal amount received

■ AU/UN Hybrid operation in Darfur (UNAMID) - budget

Awareness

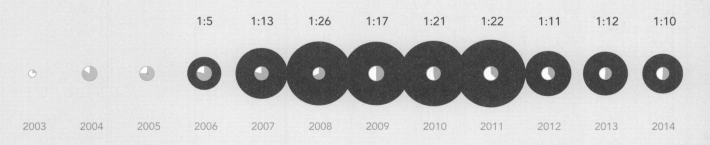

1:5   1:13   1:26   1:17   1:21   1:22   1:11   1:12   1:10

2003 2004 2005 2006 2007 2008 2009 2010 2011 2012 2013 2014

Sudan web page visits

ReliefWeb reports published on Sudan

Proportion of reports that mention Darfur

0:0 Ratio of reports published to web page visits

Overview of IDPs and settlements
December 2014

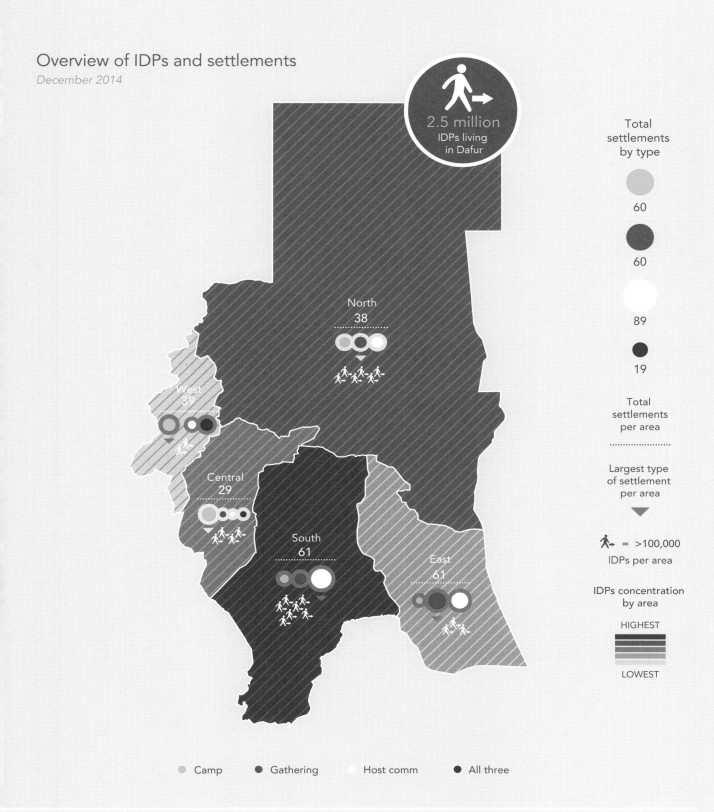

2.5 million
IDPs living
in Dafur

North
38
🚶🚶🚶

West
39
🚶🚶

Central
29
🚶🚶🚶

South
61
🚶🚶🚶🚶

East
61
🚶🚶🚶

Total
settlements
by type

60

60

89

19

Total
settlements
per area

Largest type
of settlement
per area

🚶 = >100,000
IDPs per area

IDPs concentration
by area

HIGHEST

LOWEST

● Camp   ● Gathering   ○ Host comm   ● All three

Long-term trends in natural disasters, 2004-2014

There is a lot of overlap when evaluating the top 10 countries by the number of disasters and the number of people affected by disasters. China tops the list by number of disasters (332) and number of people affected (over 1 billion). In decreasing order, the top 10 countries by number of disasters (cumulative, 2004-2014) are as follows: China, United States, the Philippines, India, Indonesia, Japan, Vietnam, Afghanistan, Mexico and Bangladesh. In decreasing order, the top 10 countries by number of people affected over the same period are as follows: China, India, the Philippines, Bangladesh, Pakistan, Thailand, Ethiopia, Kenya and the United States.

All of these countries have a national disaster management authority, but none, with the exception of Afghanistan, have made formal commitments under the Sendai Framework. The risk profiles for the countries vary widely. When broken down to compare a country's natural disaster hazard index to its overall Index for Risk Management (InfoRM, see figure's technical note), it is possible to observe indirectly the level of investment in disaster management and the country's capacity to absorb shock. For example, Japan experiences a high number of natural disasters and has a very high natural disaster hazard index (8.12). However, its overall risk profile is very low, which demonstrates good investment in its national disaster risk management. The same trend is observed in India and Mexico, among other countries. Interestingly, most of the countries with high numbers of natural disasters and/or high levels of disaster-affected people have not had an inter-agency appeal. Five countries (Afghanistan, Ethiopia, Kenya, Pakistan and the Philippines) have had multiple inter-agency appeals.

Mexico

73		RM	4.6
11.3m			7.5

United States

242		RM	3.1
20.9m			7.5

Ethiopia

37		12		RM	6.4
22.3m		31.6m			4.22

Kenya

52		6		RM	6.2
21.0m		13.1m			4.2

CRED, InfoRM, inter-agency appeal documents, ReliefWeb, UNISDR, PreventionWeb

FIGURE 17

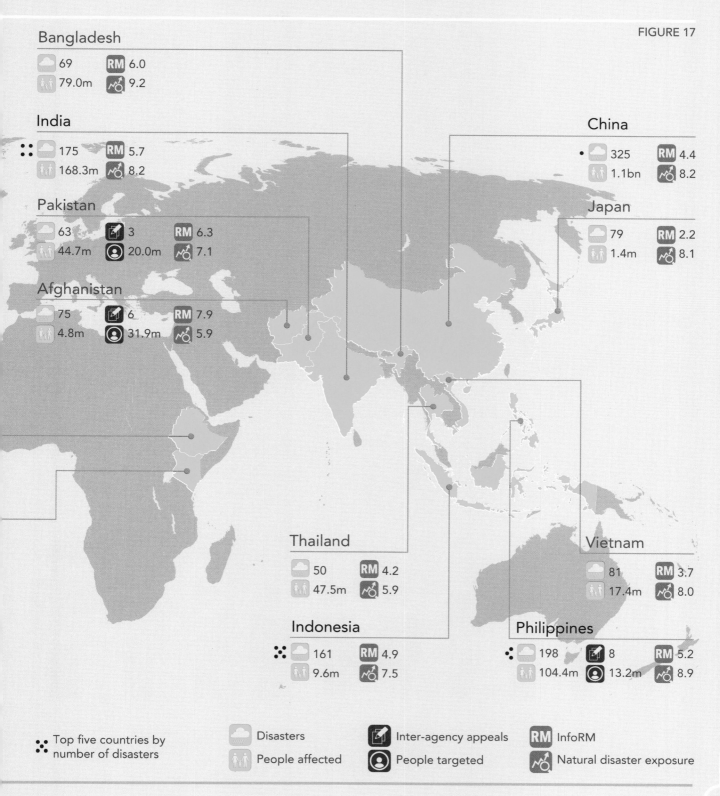

Bangladesh
- ☁ 69
- 👪 79.0m
- RM 6.0
- 📈 9.2

India
- ☁ 175
- 👪 168.3m
- RM 5.7
- 📈 8.2

Pakistan
- ☁ 63
- 👪 44.7m
- ✍ 3
- 👤 20.0m
- RM 6.3
- 📈 7.1

Afghanistan
- ☁ 75
- 👪 4.8m
- ✍ 6
- 👤 31.9m
- RM 7.9
- 📈 5.9

China
- ☁ 325
- 👪 1.1bn
- RM 4.4
- 📈 8.2

Japan
- ☁ 79
- 👪 1.4m
- RM 2.2
- 📈 8.1

Thailand
- ☁ 50
- 👪 47.5m
- RM 4.2
- 📈 5.9

Indonesia
- ☁ 161
- 👪 9.6m
- RM 4.9
- 📈 7.5

Vietnam
- ☁ 81
- 👪 17.4m
- RM 3.7
- 📈 8.0

Philippines
- ☁ 198
- 👪 104.4m
- ✍ 8
- 👤 13.2m
- RM 5.2
- 📈 8.9

Legend:
- ⋮ Top five countries by number of disasters
- ☁ Disasters
- 👪 People affected
- ✍ Inter-agency appeals
- 👤 People targeted
- RM InfoRM
- 📈 Natural disaster exposure

Long-term trends in conflict

The number of political conflicts has steadily increased since 2006 by an average of 18 conflicts per year. Most new conflicts are intra-State. On average, Asia and Oceania records the most conflicts per year (116), but sub-Saharan Africa records the most high-intensity conflicts per year (13). The number of high-intensity conflicts has decreased in all regions since 2012. The exception is in the Middle East and Maghreb, where the number of high-intensity conflicts in 2014 reached a record 14.

Conflicts per year
Number of political conflicts per type

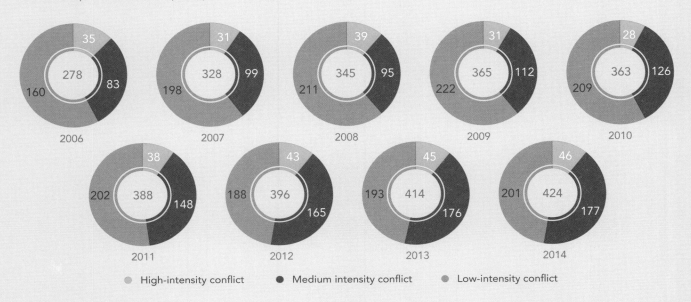

● High-intensity conflict   ● Medium intensity conflict   ● Low-intensity conflict

Number of forcibly displaced people by conflict and violence
Millions

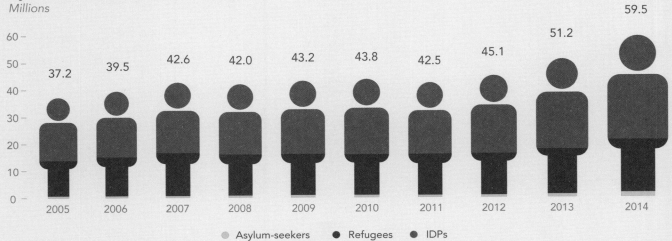

● Asylum-seekers   ● Refugees   ● IDPs

* For a brief definition of a political conflict and intensity levels, see the technical note for figure 4.
Sources: Heidelberg Institute for International Conflict Research, IDMC, UNHCR

Beyond the economic cost of conflict, currently estimated at $14.3 trillion, the human cost of conflict has continuously increased in the last 10 years. A record number of people have been forcibly displaced by conflict or violence: approximately 60 million in 2014 or the equivalent of the population of Italy. Since 2005, the number of IDPs per year has been nearly twice the number of refugees.

Number of political conflicts per region

FIGURE 18

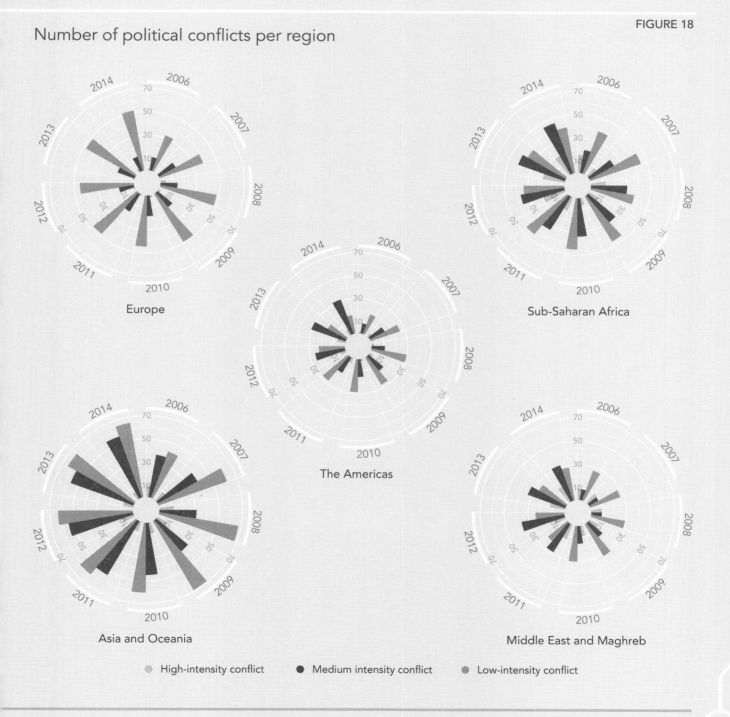

Europe

The Americas

Sub-Saharan Africa

Asia and Oceania

Middle East and Maghreb

● High-intensity conflict   ● Medium intensity conflict   ● Low-intensity conflict

Vulnerability and cycles of internal displacement

In 2014, 11 million people were newly displaced due to violence or conflict. This is equivalent to 30,000 people fleeing each day. Generally, the ratio of men to women among IDPs tends to match that of the general population, with slightly more women than men living in protracted displacement. Displacement is often recurrent and protracted, fuelled by vulnerability and the failure to secure IDPs' return, local integration or settlement elsewhere in broader development and peacebuilding programmes.

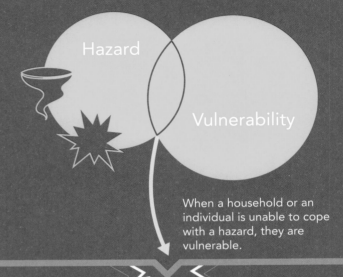

Hazard

Vulnerability

When a household or an individual is unable to cope with a hazard, they are vulnerable.

General population

Increasing numbers of IDPs flee to urban areas, where they are largely invisible

60%

5 COUNTRIES

2014

IDPs : REFUGEES

There are three types of durable solutions:
1. return
2. local integration
3. settlement elsewhere in the country.

IDPs have achieved durable solutions when they are not discriminated against and they have access to security, basic services, education, livelihoods, land, effective justice and voting rights.

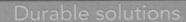

Durable solutions

Returned population

Durable solutions require a holistic approach that integrates national and international initiatives. Currently, only return is monitored by Governments and international organizations. Local integration happens incrementally and is harder to measure. The international community has developed criteria to assess whether durable solutions have been achieved, but these criteria are hard to measure.

Source: IDMC, OCHA

FIGURE 19

Vulnerability

Investing in prevention and mitigation can decrease vulnerability. For example, Japan is routinely featured among the most at-risk countries for natural disasters, yet it suffers little displacement due to its investment in national capacity.

Displacement can exert a particularly heavy toll on children. Displaced children generally no longer attend school, and often their food needs are no longer met. They may be separated from their families during conflict or their flight, which makes them particularly vulnerable to exploitation.

The pre-existing vulnerabilities of single-female households and widows are also exacerbated by displacement.

In 20 countries, people who have been displaced once have fled again to escape additional violence in their place of refuge

Displacement

Stalled solutions

Living in displacement for **10**yrs or more 2014

IN

90% of **60** countries and territories

Role of aid programmes

The way international humanitarian and development actors respond today lays the foundation for tomorrow's vulnerability. Recovery and development strategies have created "stalled" solutions, mainly due to the inability to address specific needs, poor support for national capacities, lack of funding and lack of adequate programming (promoting social and economic recovery, protection/security/ rule of law, governance and social cohesion).

Disaster-related displacement and middle-income countries

In 2014, 19.3 million people were displaced by natural disasters. Ninety-one per cent of this displacement was due to weather-related events. The three countries with the highest numbers of disaster-induced displacement were China, India and the Philippines. They also had the highest levels of cumulative displacement for the 2008-2014 period. All three countries have experienced repeating patterns of displacement, with floods and storms regularly causing the most displacement in these three countries.

60%
China
India
Philippines

Disaster displacement
2008-2014

19.3 million people

Displaced by disasters in 2014

An average of **22.5 million** people have been displaced each year by weather-related disasters since 2008 equivalent to **62,000 people every day**

8/20 largest disasters by numbers of displaced were caused by typhoons or tropical storms in Asia

91%

Displacement caused by weather-related events in 2014

Urban population trends
Billions

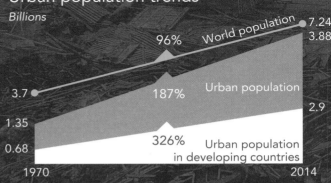

7.24
3.88

96%   World population

3.7

1.35

0.68

187%   Urban population   2.9

326%   Urban population in developing countries

1970   2014

Global displacement and population by income group

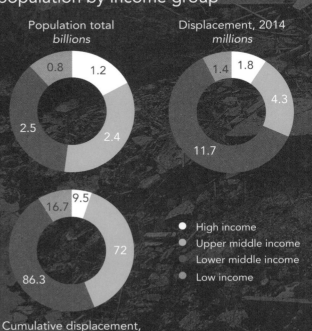

Population total
billions

0.8   1.2

2.5   2.4

Displacement, 2014
millions

1.4   1.8

4.3

11.7

16.7   9.5

72

86.3

- High income
- Upper middle income
- Lower middle income
- Low income

Cumulative displacement, 2008–2014, *millions*

Sources: CRED EM-DAT, IDMC, UN Statistics Division, World Bank

China, India and the Philippines are middle-income countries with growing economies and growing urban populations. Many of these new urban dwellers are drawn to economic centres for job opportunities. This causes unchecked development in cities, which, in turn, increases their exposure to natural hazards. Without adequate prevention-and-mitigation measures, many of these urban dwellers have high levels of vulnerability. All three countries have a natural disaster management authority and have invested in their national capacities for risk management, evidenced by the large numbers of disaster-affected people who are not displaced (see figure 17). However, uncontrolled urbanization will continue to be a key driver of exposure and vulnerability.

FIGURE 20

Displacement in China, Philippines, India, 2008 to 2014

China

		2008	2009	2010	2011	2012	2013	2014
Number of disasters		30	26	26	20	28	42	40
Affected people (millions)		137	128	181	124	45	27	65
People displaced by natural disasters (millions)		19	4	16	4	6	6	3
GDP per capita (current US$)		$3,441	$3,800	$4,515	$5,574	$6,265	$6,992	$7,594
Urban population (per cent)			53%	52%	51%	50%	48%	47%

India

		2008	2009	2010	2011	2012	2013	2014
Number of disasters		11	17	19	13	10	12	15
Affected people (millions)		14	11	4	13	4	17	6
People displaced by natural disasters (millions)		6	5	2	2	9	2	3
GDP per capita (current US$)		$1,023	$1,125	$1,388	$1,472	$1,450	$1,455	$1,596
Urban population (per cent)		29%			31%			

Philippines

		2008	2009	2010	2011	2012	2013	2014
Number of disasters		20	25	15	36	22	14	13
Affected people (millions)		8	13	5	12	12	25	13
People displaced by natural disasters (millions)		3	2	1	2	4	7	6
GDP per capita (current US$)		$1,929	$1,837	$2,145	$2,372	$2,606	$2,788	$2,871

The impact of explosive weapons on civilian populations

The use of explosive weapons in populated areas is a major cause of death, injuries, damage and displacement to civilians due to their wide-area impact. Between 2011 and 2014, 144,545 deaths and injuries were recorded from the use of explosive weapons. Of these deaths and injuries, 78 per cent were civilians. During this same period, 10,386 incidents were recorded. Sixty per cent of these incidents took place in populated areas, and 90 per cent of deaths and injuries in populated areas were civilians. Between 2011 and 2014, there were 77 civilian deaths and injuries per day and 23 civilian fatalities per day on average.

Weapons most used in populated areas

158 Incidents
ARTILLERY SHELL
10

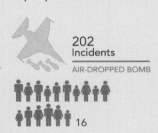

202 Incidents
AIR-DROPPED BOMB
16

249 Incidents
SHELLING
9

Average civilian deaths and injuries per incident

318 Incidents
MULTIPLE EXPLOSIVE WEAPONS
24

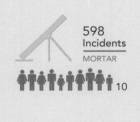

598 Incidents
MORTAR
10

92 countries and territories have reported incidents of explosive violence

Average civilian deaths and injuries per incident

690 Incidents
GRENADE
6

932 Incidents
CAR BOMB
24

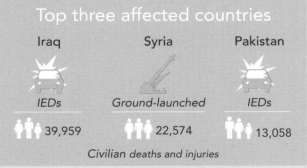

Top three affected countries

Iraq	Syria	Pakistan
IEDs	Ground-launched	IEDs
39,959	22,574	13,058

Civilian deaths and injuries

Source: Action on Armed Violence.

FIGURE 21

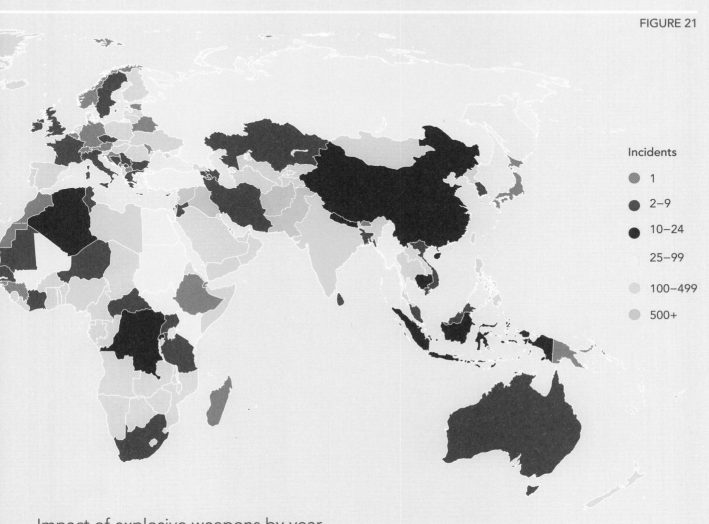

Incidents

- 1
- 2–9
- 10–24
- 25–99
- 100–499
- 500+

Impact of explosive weapons by year

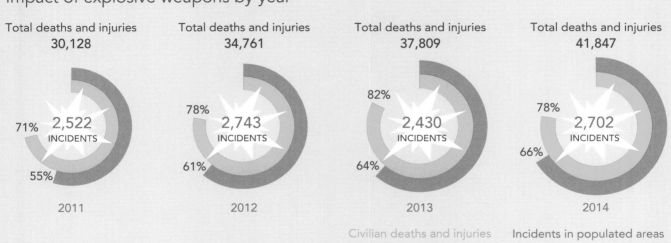

Total deaths and injuries
30,128

71%   2,522
INCIDENTS
55%

2011

Total deaths and injuries
34,761

78%   2,743
INCIDENTS
61%

2012

Total deaths and injuries
37,809

82%   2,430
INCIDENTS
64%

2013

Total deaths and injuries
41,847

78%   2,702
INCIDENTS
66%

2014

Civilian deaths and injuries   Incidents in populated areas

The use of improvised explosive devices

IEDs include a range of makeshift explosive weapons. They can be made from military ordnance, commercial explosives or common homemade sources. IED attacks kill and injure thousands of civilians each year, damage homes and infrastructure, and undermine the security and development of affected communities. Between 2011 and 2014, IED incidents were recorded in 71 countries. On average, 78 per cent of IED casualties were civilians. Suicide bombings, a type of IED attack,

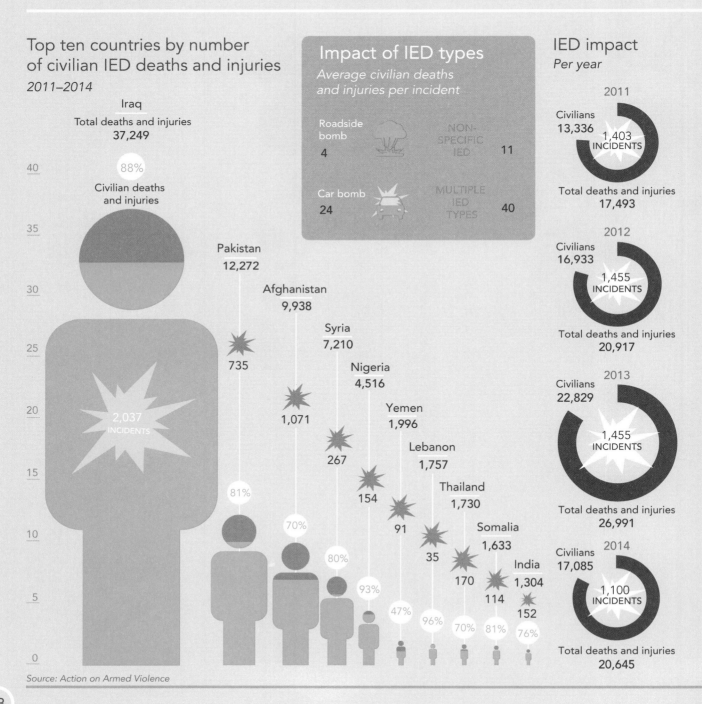

Top ten countries by number of civilian IED deaths and injuries
2011–2014

Iraq
Total deaths and injuries
37,249

40

88%

Civilian deaths and injuries

35

30

25

2,037
INCIDENTS

20

15

Pakistan
12,272

Afghanistan
9,938

735

Syria
7,210

1,071

Nigeria
4,516

267

81%

70%

Yemen
1,996

154

80%

Lebanon
1,757

91

93%

Thailand
1,730

35

Somalia
1,633

170

47%

India
1,304

114

152

96%

70%

81%

76%

10

5

0

Source: Action on Armed Violence

Impact of IED types
Average civilian deaths and injuries per incident

Roadside bomb
4

NON-SPECIFIC IED **11**

Car bomb
24

MULTIPLE IED TYPES **40**

IED impact
Per year

2011
Civilians
13,336
1,403 INCIDENTS
Total deaths and injuries
17,493

2012
Civilians
16,933
1,455 INCIDENTS
Total deaths and injuries
20,917

2013
Civilians
22,829
1,455 INCIDENTS
Total deaths and injuries
26,991

2014
Civilians
17,085
1,100 INCIDENTS
Total deaths and injuries
20,645

were recorded in 29 countries between 2011 and 2014. During this period, there was a 28 per cent increase in the number of suicide attacks, with civilians constituting nearly 35 per cent of deaths and injuries.

In this worsening landscape, practical policies to disrupt access to IED materials and bomb-making knowledge need to be implemented nationally and internationally. Victims of this form of violence should receive a full range of support, including treatment for psychological harm.

Impact of suicide bombings
Per year

FIGURE 22

Top ten countries by number of civilian deaths and injuries from suicide bombings
2011–2014

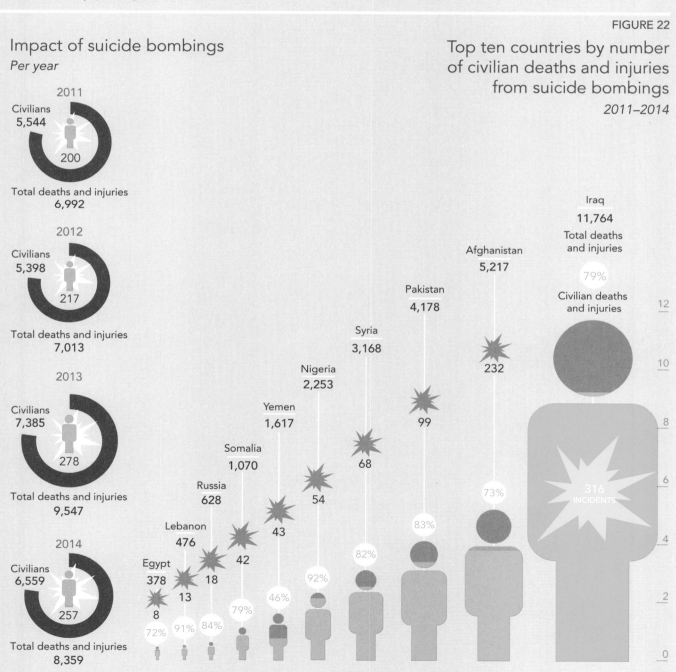

2011
Civilians 5,544
200
Total deaths and injuries 6,992

2012
Civilians 5,398
217
Total deaths and injuries 7,013

2013
Civilians 7,385
278
Total deaths and injuries 9,547

2014
Civilians 6,559
257
Total deaths and injuries 8,359

Egypt 378 — 8 — 72%
Lebanon 476 — 13 — 91%
Russia 628 — 18 — 84%
Somalia 1,070 — 42 — 79%
Yemen 1,617 — 43 — 46%
Nigeria 2,253 — 54 — 92%
Syria 3,168 — 68 — 82%
Pakistan 4,178 — 99 — 83%
Afghanistan 5,217 — 232 — 73%
Iraq 11,764 — Total deaths and injuries — 79% — Civilian deaths and injuries — 316 INCIDENTS

Challenges

The data deficit: the case of East Africa

Accurate data is crucial in humanitarian response. Data contributes to planning processes by showing gaps in national capacities, supporting rapid decisions by reflecting humanitarian need and providing the evidence base for advocacy. Lack of data has implications for gaining an accurate understanding of regional vulnerability. OCHA's Humanitarian Data Exchange (HDX) team established a Data Lab in Nairobi, Kenya, in 2014 to offer data services to partners and connect data from across the region. One of its first projects was a data-hunting exercise to collect information on 43 indicators at the state level across 10 countries (Burundi, Djibouti, Eritrea, Ethiopia, Kenya, Rwanda, Somalia, Sudan, South Sudan and Uganda).

	Security incidents	Schooling (% of population)	Multi-Dimensional Poverty Index	Integrated phase classification	Drinking water (% of population)	Deprived of improved sanitation (% of population)	Access to electricity	Surface area (sq. km)	Population	Poverty headcount ratio, below $1.25/day	Child mortality, % of population	Violent conflict probability	Total affected by drought	Road density	Returned refugees	Remittances as a % of GDP	Refugees who are assisted by UNHCR	Refugees, by country of asylum	Physicians density	Physical exposure to flood
East Africa	●	●	●	●	●	●	●	●	●	●	●	●	●	●	●	●	●	●	●	●
Uganda	●	●	●	●	●	●	●	●	●	●	●	●	●	●	●	●	●	○	●	●
Sudan	●	○	○	●	●	●	○	●	●	●	●	●	●	○	●	●	●	●	●	●
South Sudan	●	●	●	●	●	●	●	●	●	●	●	●	●	●	○	●	●	○	●	●
Somalia	●	●	●	●	●	●	●	●	●	○	●	●	○	●	●	●	●	●	●	●
Rwanda	●	●	●	●	●	●	●	●	●	●	●	●	●	●	●	●	●	○	●	●
Kenya	●	●	●	●	●	●	●	●	●	●	●	●	●	●	●	●	●	●	○	●
Ethiopia	●	●	●	●	●	●	●	●	●	●	●	●	●	●	●	●	●	○	●	●
Eritrea	●	○	○	●	●	●	●	●	●	○	●	●	●	●	●	●	○	○	●	●
Djibouti	●	●	○	●	●	●	●	●	●	○	●	●	●	○	●	●	●	○	●	●
Burundi	●	●	●	●	●	●	●	●	●	●	●	●	●	●	●	●	●	○	●	●

Source: Humanitarian Data Exchange

The data covered topics such as livelihoods, health conditions, infrastructure and population displacement. Data sources included Government ministries, UN agencies, the World Bank and the private sector. Over a three-month period, the data lab conducted physical and virtual outreach in search of the data. Data was manually extracted from static maps, GIS files, PDF documents and Excel spreadsheets. About 25 percent of the data collected was considered 'complete', meaning there was data at the national and sub-national levels for every state in a specific country. No single indicator was available across all 10 countries at a sub-national level. The exercise showed the challenges contributing to the data divide: data is either not being collected or, when it is, is not shared in an accessible format.

FIGURE 23

Complete · Partial · National · No data

Online volunteer coordination: the Ebola emergency

The 2014-2015 Ebola virus disease outbreak devastated West Africa. As of 1 July 2015, 27,524 cases and 11,228 deaths had been recorded in Guinea, Liberia and Sierra Leone. Responders were tested by the scale of the emergency, the urban setting and underresourced national infrastructures. The speed of sharing data and information was recognized as key in containing the spread of the disease. The crisis also demonstrated the importance of partnering with non-traditional actors and embracing innovative methods to collect data, such as crowdsourcing and online coordination. A group of online volunteers, led by the Standby Task Force (SBTF), compiled information on health-care facilities. The information was then mapped out with the support of OCHA and UN Mission for Ebola Emergency Response (UNMEER) and released to relevant responders.

Online volunteer coordination – how does it work?

Step 1: Identifying reliable situational information

- SBTF used information published on local blogs, newspapers, NGO social media sites, and embassy/company websites.

- Identified 170 organizations responding to the crisis in various capacities and sectors, and compiled a comprehensive list of journalists, tweeters and information sources.

CHALLENGES
Gathering information
- The complexity of collection (outdated or unverifiable information)
- Inaccessibility of existing data
- High volume of information.

CHALLENGES
Sharing information
- Dilemma between open and closed sharing of information. For example, contact information for local offices could not be made publically available as it could not always be verified.

- Members of the humanitarian community initiated Skype conversations to enable information sharing. The main Skype group included 232 active participants, representing 101 NGOs, international organizations, Government actors (foreign and domestic) and volunteer technical communities.

- A resource hub was generated using Google Sheets.

Step 2: Initial contact with key organizations/facilitating communities

CHALLENGES
Online collaboration
- Limitations using Google Sheets: The program did not allow for efficient sorting and annotating large volumes of information and links.
- Limited participation: In the IM/GIS chat, for example, 15 per cent of participating organizations provided 77.6 per cent of the posts.

OVERALL CHALLENGE

The coordination of volunteers was done by SBTF and DHN volunteers until December 2014, when a coordinator was funded in part through OCHA. The size of the operation required full-time moderation. This was a key lesson learnt: coordination is important, but it can place a lot of strain on the volunteer community without adequate support.

Source: Digital Humanitarian Network, HDx, Standby Task Force

From August 2014 until March 2015, volunteers gathered information on organizations active on the ground, and baseline data on geography, infrastructure, health facilities and more. SBTF was involved in coordinating the online community, where more than 100 organizations collaborated. They deployed about 200 volunteers. The resulting map of health-care infrastructure facilitated responders' work by offering information about existing national capacities. The online collaboration showed the value of cooperation and information exchange between responders and the volunteer digital community. The initiative also revealed the need for a mutual understanding of working methods, suitable tasking for the volunteer digital community, and the challenges in data sourcing and sharing.

FIGURE 24

- The Digital Humanitarian Network (DHN) put out an expanded call to multiple organizations. This resulted in 195 volunteers signing up to help collect information on health facilities in Guinea, Liberia and Sierra Leone.

Step 3: **Call for volunteers for data collection on facilities**

CHALLENGES
Collecting contact information
- Difficulties identifying current contact information as some websites were no longer available or precise street addresses were non existent.
- In Liberia, identifying organizations outside of Monrovia proved difficult as most databases listed only Monrovia addresses.

CHALLENGES
Coordinating volunteers
- Lack of a significant group of leaders to direct 195 volunteers.
- The global spread of volunteers required coordinators to work around the clock to accommodate different time zones .

Step 4: **Data analysis and reporting**

- Volunteers collected, compiled, geolocated and partly verified a list of almost 5,000 health facilities.
- The data came from open sources on the Internet as well as official records of clinics, hospitals and individual private practices.
- All information was shared on the Humanitarian Data Exchange platform.

Step 5: **Enabling communication with local organizations**

- The NetHope Ebola Response Program aimed to install internet technology in selected NGOs operating in Sierra Leone and Liberia.
- SBTF members created a database of 220 NGOs that NetHope could contact to possibly install communication hardware.

Opportunities

Innovative tools for data coordination and collection

Technology is driving new (often inexpensive) modalities for information sharing and communication in humanitarian response. On 27 August 2014, members of the humanitarian community began the Ebola IM/GIS Skype group. This platform enabled communications across agencies and countries to share best practices and latest news in information management (IM) and geospatial information systems (GIS) during the Ebola response. The group was formed under the overall coordination of the Digital Humanitarian Network (DHN). Between August 2014 and May 2015, 232 people

Use of Skype

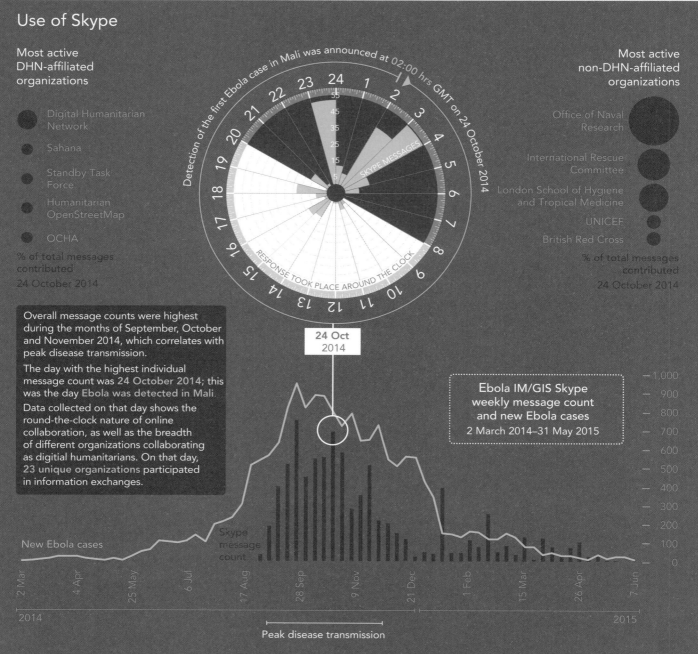

Most active DHN-affiliated organizations

- Digital Humanitarian Network
- Sahana
- Standby Task Force
- Humanitarian OpenStreetMap
- OCHA

% of total messages contributed
24 October 2014

Most active non-DHN-affiliated organizations

- Office of Naval Research
- International Rescue Committee
- London School of Hygiene and Tropical Medicine
- UNICEF
- British Red Cross

% of total messages contributed
24 October 2014

Detection of the first Ebola case in Mali was announced at 02:00 hrs GMT on 24 October 2014

SKYPE MESSAGES

RESPONSE TOOK PLACE AROUND THE CLOCK

24 Oct 2014

Overall message counts were highest during the months of September, October and November 2014, which correlates with peak disease transmission.

The day with the highest individual message count was 24 October 2014; this was the day Ebola was detected in Mali.

Data collected on that day shows the round-the-clock nature of online collaboration, as well as the breadth of different organizations collaborating as digitial humanitarians. On that day, 23 unique organizations participated in information exchanges.

Ebola IM/GIS Skype weekly message count and new Ebola cases
2 March 2014–31 May 2015

New Ebola cases

Skype message count

Peak disease transmission

2 Mar | 4 Apr | 25 May | 6 Jul | 17 Aug | 28 Sep | 9 Nov | 21 Dec | 1 Feb | 15 Mar | 26 Apr | 7 Jun

2014

2015

1,000 900 800 700 600 500 400 300 200 100 0

Source: Digital Humanitarian Network, Harvard Humanitarian Initiative, KoBoToolbox

representing 101 organizations were active within the Skype group. On average, there were more non-DHN-affiliated organizations active each month than DHN-affiliated organizations (e.g. OCHA and WHO). This suggests that while there is external interest in contribution to humanitarian response, digital humanitarians do not engage in an environment independent of formal humanitarian agencies. The Ebola IM/GIS group shows how technology creates opportunities for humanitarian agencies to engage with new collaborators.

KoBoToolbox: overview of users, projects and submissions

FIGURE 25

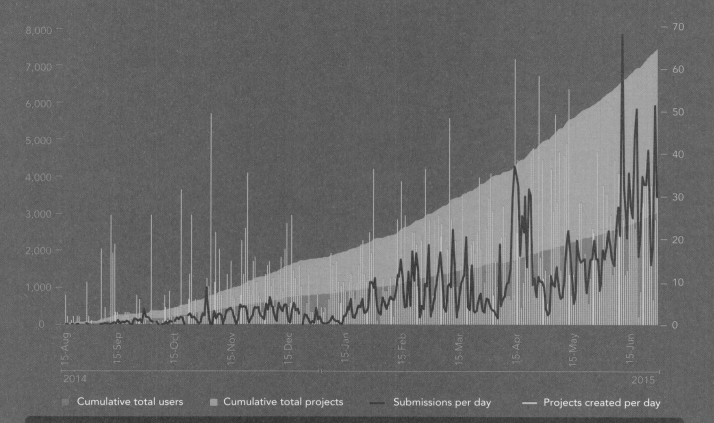

- ■ Cumulative total users
- ■ Cumulative total projects
- — Submissions per day
- — Projects created per day

KoBoToolbox

KoBoToolbox is a suite of tools for field-data collection for use in challenging environments. The platform was launched in August 2014. In just eight months, more than 3,000 users have registered, over 4,000 survey projects have been created and nearly 300,000 responses have been submitted. The advantages of a user-friendly, open-source tool were evident following the Nepal earthquake (25 April 2015). Following the earthquake, the Harvard Humanitarian Initiative sent a data-collection specialist to support OCHA with humanitarian needs assessments. Local and international partners decided to conduct the first comprehensive needs assessment in Sindhupalchok—the most affected district. Within 72 hours of this decision being made, an assessment team comprising 25 volunteers from local NGOs was assembled, trained and dispatched to the field on 11 May 2015 to collect data based on key informant interviews. The assessment form was created in coordination with each cluster and converted into the electronic KoBoToolbox format on the ground. It was later used in other districts. A record 7,863 survey submissions were received on a single day (11 June 2015). The use of an online platform greatly facilitated assessments by providing a template for data collectors and the capacity to share results in real-time and perform quick analysis.

Social media and humanitarian disasters: Typhoon Ruby

During humanitarian crises, social media users around the world post messages, photos and videos to various social media sites. The use of social media as a means for communication and a place to gather data remains an experimental field for humanitarian organizations. However, mainstream media have embraced the phenomenon and routinely feature user-generated content in articles and broadcasts. Given the large volume, velocity and variety of information contained in social media sites, capturing relevant data requires a significant amount of processing. Technologies for processing and aggregating those messages through a mixture of computing algorithms and human annotations have continued to mature in recent years.

Types of tweets

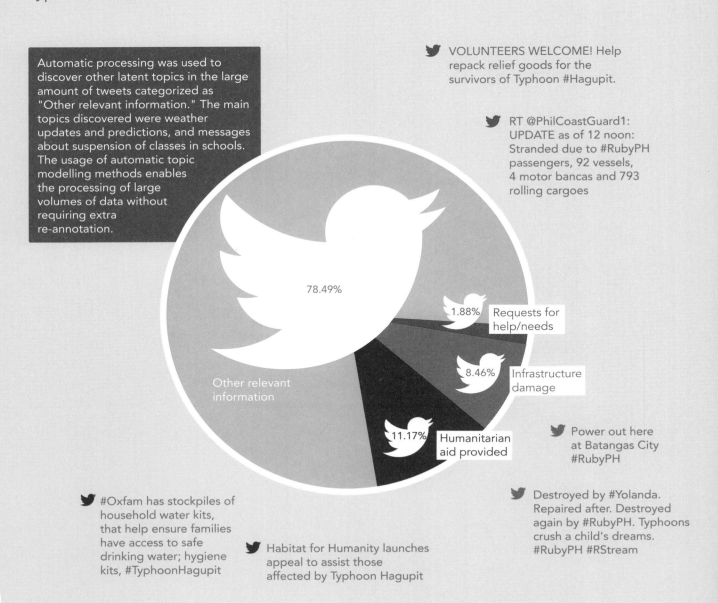

Automatic processing was used to discover other latent topics in the large amount of tweets categorized as "Other relevant information." The main topics discovered were weather updates and predictions, and messages about suspension of classes in schools. The usage of automatic topic modelling methods enables the processing of large volumes of data without requiring extra re-annotation.

VOLUNTEERS WELCOME! Help repack relief goods for the survivors of Typhoon #Hagupit.

RT @PhilCoastGuard1: UPDATE as of 12 noon: Stranded due to #RubyPH passengers, 92 vessels, 4 motor bancas and 793 rolling cargoes

78.49%

Other relevant information

1.88%   Requests for help/needs

8.46%   Infrastructure damage

11.17%   Humanitarian aid provided

Power out here at Batangas City #RubyPH

#Oxfam has stockpiles of household water kits, that help ensure families have access to safe drinking water; hygiene kits, #TyphoonHagupit

Habitat for Humanity launches appeal to assist those affected by Typhoon Hagupit

Destroyed by #Yolanda. Repaired after. Destroyed again by #RubyPH. Typhoons crush a child's dreams. #RubyPH #RStream

Source: Qatar Computing Research Institute, MicroMappers

The Philippines has a large population of active social media users, and their response to Typhoon Hagupit (Ruby) on December 2014 was similar to the response for Super Typhoon Haiyan (Yolanda) in November 2013, with hundreds of thousands of messages posted to various sites. During the Typhoon Ruby response, approximately 700 digital volunteers classified Twitter messages through the MicroMappers.org interface during approximately 72 hours. In total, 12,628 tweets were categorized. Among the relevant tweets, over 10 per cent related to humanitarian aid and approximately 2 per cent were requests for help.

Geo-location of tweets and images

FIGURE 26

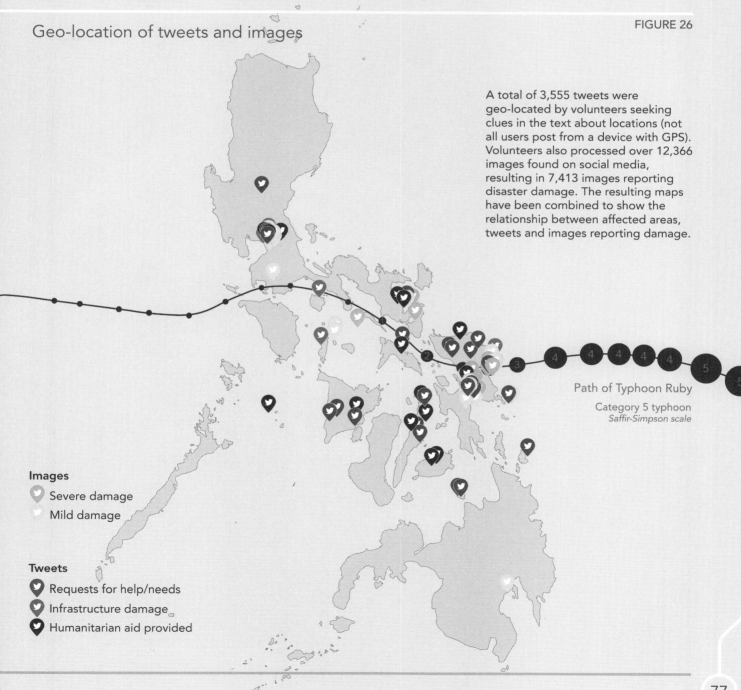

A total of 3,555 tweets were geo-located by volunteers seeking clues in the text about locations (not all users post from a device with GPS). Volunteers also processed over 12,366 images found on social media, resulting in 7,413 images reporting disaster damage. The resulting maps have been combined to show the relationship between affected areas, tweets and images reporting damage.

Path of Typhoon Ruby
Category 5 typhoon
Saffir-Simpson scale

Images
- Severe damage
- Mild damage

Tweets
- Requests for help/needs
- Infrastructure damage
- Humanitarian aid provided

Perceptions about humanitarian action

The World Humanitarian Summit is an initiative of the UN Secretary-General. It is the first global summit on humanitarian action of this size and scope, and it will be held in Istanbul in May 2016. Its goal is to bring the global community together to commit to new ways of working together to save lives and reduce hardship around the globe. In the two years leading up to the summit, regional consultations and surveys were conducted to gather perspectives, priorities and recommendations from all stakeholders on what must be done to make

humanitarian action fit for the future. The questions and answers in this infographic were featured in these surveys. They present a snapshot of global perceptions about humanitarian action.

TOPIC: DIASPORA

What is your diaspora's role in emergency assistance/preparedness in your country of origin?

food assistance

advocacy and
raising funds   **support**

water and medical assistance

sending funds
emergency assistance

TOPIC: YOUTH

Where can young people contribute to humanitarian assistance?

education

development

delivering services   social media

awareness

engaging

Source: World Humanitarian Summit Secretariat

FIGURE 27

TOPIC: PRIVATE SECTOR

What are the barriers for private sector support in emergencies?

Logistical challenges/access

Cost effectiveness

Unsure who coordinates response

- Eastern and Southern Africa
- Latin America and the Caribbean
- Middle East and North Africa

TOPIC: COOPERATION

What are the main challenges for agencies to respond impartially in conflict?

safety and security of staff

concerns over host community backlash

government restrictions

lack of access

lack of funding

TOPIC: INNOVATION

Which areas have the most potential to improve emergency response?

Improved use of ICTs (mobile phones, internet and social media)

Improved logistics

Better communication/participation of affected communities

- Eastern and Southern Africa
- Latin America and the Caribbean
- Middle East and North Africa

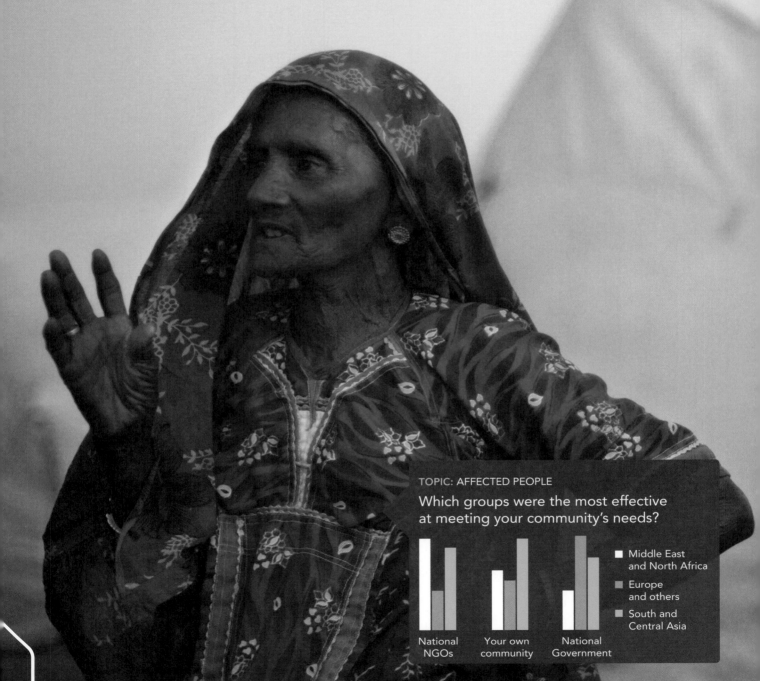

TOPIC: AFFECTED PEOPLE

Which groups were the most effective
at meeting your community's needs?

National
NGOs

Your own
community

National
Government

■ Middle East
and North Africa

■ Europe
and others

■ South and
Central Asia

TOPIC: PREPAREDNESS AND PREVENTION

Who has the main responsibility for helping
to prepare for/prevent crises?

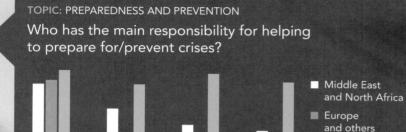

■ Middle East
and North Africa

■ Europe
and others

■ South and
Central Asia

The
Government

Local aid
groups

Your own
community

International
aid groups

TOPIC: MILITARY COORDINATION

What has prevented your organization
from coordinating with other
aid groups?

logistical barriers

information
not shared

political
complexities

humanitarian system is unwelcoming

limited capacity

TOPIC: RESILIENCE

What are the biggest obstacles
to integrating risk management
and reducing vulnerability
into operations?

insufficient
technical
capacity

lack of information about
risks and vulnerablilities

multiple risks make
interventions complicated

lack political commitment

lack of financial resources

USER'S GUIDE

User's Guide

Limitations

This report is intended to provide a comprehensive overview of global humanitarian data and trends. However, there are many gaps and inconsistencies in the information available. There is no single, comprehensive source of humanitarian information and data. There are no widely used standards for measuring humanitarian needs or response, even less so for measuring the long-term effectiveness of assistance. And there are no agreed definitions of humanitarian needs or assistance.

Humanitarian emergencies and their drivers are extremely complex. By definition, crises are chaotic. They arise due to the interrelationships between multiple causes, which are not easily measured or understood. Political and practical difficulties can prevent the collection and sharing of information about humanitarian needs and assistance. Humanitarian assistance involves a plethora of actors, from affected people and communities to local and national Governments, civil society and international aid organizations. Organizations account for what they do in varying ways, and the efforts of many actors are not reported at all. Some humanitarian actors may not be willing or able to share the information they collect, which often leads to biases or gaps in the information available.

There are also technical limitations that affect the availability, consistency, reliability and comparability of data. There is a lack of common standards for data and sharing protocols, and statistical systems in many countries are still weak. Statistical methods, coverage, practices and definitions differ widely. Comparison between countries and across time zones involves complex technical and conceptual problems that cannot be resolved easily or unequivocally. Data coverage may not be complete because of special circumstances affecting the collection and reporting of data, such as problems arising from conflicts. These factors are more prominent in countries that are experiencing or vulnerable to major humanitarian emergencies.

Because of these limitations, the data presented in this report should only be interpreted to indicate major trends and characterize major differences between emergencies and countries. Readers should consult the original sources for detailed information on the limitations of the data.

Technical notes

Countries

The term "country" refers to any territory for which authorities or other organizations report separate statistics. It does not necessarily imply political independence.

Regions and country groupings

Regional groupings are based on the World Bank's classification of major world regions: East Asia and Pacific, Europe and Central Asia, Latin America and the Caribbean, Middle East and North Africa, South Asia, and sub-Saharan Africa.

Income groups are based on the World Bank's classification http://data.worldbank.org/about/country-classifications. Countries are divided according to annual GNI per capita, calculated using the *World Bank Atlas* method. In 2014, these income cut-offs are low income, US$1,045 or less; lower-middle income, $1,046–$4,125; upper-middle income, $4,126 - $12,736; and high income, $12,736 or more. Low-income and lower-middle-income countries are sometimes referred to as "developing countries".

Humanitarian funding

Humanitarian aid/humanitarian assistance – This includes the aid and actions designed to save lives, alleviate suffering, and maintain and protect human dignity during and following emergencies. The characteristics that separate this from other forms of assistance are 1) it is intended to be governed by the principles of humanity, neutrality, impartiality and independence; 2) it is intended to be short term in nature and provide for activities during and in the immediate aftermath of an emergency. In practice, these phases are difficult to define, especially in protracted emergencies or situations of chronic vulnerability. Humanitarian aid can also include risk reduction, preparedness activities and recovery. Humanitarian aid is given by Governments, individuals, NGOs, multilateral organizations, domestic organizations and private companies. Different actors have different definitions of "humanitarian", and some may not differentiate humanitarian aid from other forms of assistance. For the purposes of this report, aid is considered to be humanitarian if it is reported as such by the actor that provides it.

Humanitarian aid contributions from Governments in this report include:

1. The humanitarian aid expenditures using data from the OECD DAC and FTS. The 29 OECD DAC members[1] and some non-members report annually on Official Development Assistance (ODA) flows to OECD. Reports include bilateral humanitarian aid contributions plus ODA flows to multinational organizations.

2. Funding through inter-agency appeals reported by donors to FTS. Data is in current prices.

Official Development Assistance – This comprises a grant or loan from an official source to a developing country (as defined by OECD) or multilateral agency (as defined by OECD) to promote economic development and welfare. It is reported by DAC members, along with several other Government donors and institutions, according to strict criteria. Humanitarian aid typically accounts for about 10 per cent of total ODA each year.

Humanitarian inter-agency appeals

To raise money for humanitarian activities, humanitarian organizations often issue appeals or strategic response plans (post-2013). Appeals may contain information on the number of people affected by emergencies and their needs, the proposed activities to respond to those needs and the funding required. To respond to ongoing crises or after a major emergency, humanitarian organizations may participate in an inter-agency appeal process. This brings aid organizations together to jointly plan, coordinate, implement and monitor their emergency response. At the country level, the Humanitarian Coordinator leads the process, in collaboration with the Humanitarian Country Team. Types of inter-agency appeals include:

1. Strategic response plans (formerly known as consolidated appeals), which are used when several organizations appeal together for funds for the same crisis. Aid organizations use the strategic response process to plan, coordinate, fund, implement and monitor their activities. A strategic response plan can be issued for one year or more. Projects included can be planned for more than a year, but their budgets must be broken into 12-month periods.

2. Flash appeals, which are used to structure a coordinated humanitarian response for the first three to six months of an emergency. Flash appeals are issued within one week of an emergency and are triggered by the Humanitarian Coordinator in consultation with all stakeholders. The appeal provides a concise overview of urgent life-saving needs and may include recovery projects that can be implemented within the appeal's time frame.

For the purposes of this report, the term "inter-agency appeals" is used to denote, interchangeably, consolidated appeals, strategic response plans, flash appeals and other appeals that follow similar principles and processes (such as joint Government-UN plans). See **www.humanitarianresponse.info/programme-cycle/space**.

Years, symbols and conventions

- 2014 is the most recent year for which complete data was available at the time of publication. Where 2014 data is not available, the latest year is shown and this is noted.

- A dash (-) means that data is not available or that aggregates cannot be calculated because of missing data in the years shown.

- 0 or 0.0 means zero or small enough that the number would round to zero at the number of decimal places shown.

- A billion is 1,000 million.

---

1 Australia, Austria, Belgium, Canada, Czech Republic, Denmark, Finland, France, Germany, Greece, Iceland, Ireland, Italy, Japan, Korea, Luxembourg, the Netherlands, New Zealand, Norway, Poland, Portugal, Slovak Republic, Slovenia, Spain, Sweden, Switzerland, the United Kingdom, the United States and the European institutions

Technical notes by figure

The year in review 2014

Humanitarian assistance in 2014

Figure 1. The overall number of people targeted for assistance through inter-agency appeals is derived from the *Global Humanitarian Overview: Status Report August 2014*. This number is different from numbers reported in the *Global Humanitarian Assistance Report 2015* and the *Global Overview of Humanitarian Needs 2014*, as there are variations in the data used for those analyses. The number of people forcibly displaced by violence and conflict reflects the findings contained in UNHCR's annual Global Trends Report (2014) and IDMC's *Global Overview 2015: People internally displaced by conflict or violence* and *Global Estimates 2015: People internally displaced by disasters*. The number of people affected by natural disasters is sourced from the Centre for Research on the Epidemiology of Disasters International Disaster Database (CRED EM-DAT). Funding figures for international humanitarian assistance reflect the findings of the *Global Humanitarian Assistance Report 2015*.

Humanitarian needs – inter-agency appeals, funding and visibility

Figure 2. The numbers for this figure are derived from crisis-specific midyear reviews or the *Global Humanitarian Overview: Status Report August 2014* (whichever was most recent), with the exception of Afghanistan, Cameroon, DRC, Djibouti, Haiti, oPt, Sahel Region, Syria Humanitarian Response Plan and Yemen, where no midyear review was available. Figures for these countries were taken from the original planning documents. The figure for 'People to receive help/people targeted' for Cameroon was taken from the sectoral response plans contained in the *Strategic Response Plan 2014-2016*. Any discrepancies in figures are due to rounding up/down. Data for funding received was sourced from FTS. The amounts under the heading 'Funding per targeted person' were calculated using data from FTS (data captured 1 August 2015) divided by 'people targeted'.

Original planning for the Syria Regional Response Plan (RRP) predicted 4.1 million refugees by the end of 2014. An additional 2.7 million people in host communities would also benefit from the RRP. This report uses the actual number of refugees registered and assisted by UNHCR by the end of 2014, i.e., 3.9 million plus the 2.7 million people envisioned to receive help in host communities.

The level of attention an appeal receives was derived using data from ReliefWeb, namely by calculating the ratio between the number of reports published on a particular country to the number of web page visits for that country. This metric is merely an approximation of public interest, since it is based on a single source (ReliefWeb), albeit a prime information source for humanitarian practitioners.

Humanitarian needs – sector funding

Figure 3. Sectors are reflective of the 'Criteria for inclusion of reported humanitarian contributions into the Financial Tracking Service database, and for donor/appealing agency reporting to FTS'. Full descriptions of the sectors and activities are at http://fts.unocha.org/exception-docs/AboutFTS/FTS_criteria_for_posting_contributions.pdf.

For CERF funding, logistics, support services and telecoms have been folded into the overall Coordination and Support Services sector. For all funding, coordination support services - other, logistics and the UN Humanitarian Air Service have been folded into the overall Coordination and Support Services sector. Camp management has been folded into Shelter and NFI. The Health sector includes nutrition.

Conflict in 2014

Figure 4. The number of highly violent political conflicts is defined per the methodology used in the Conflict Barometer of the Heidelberg Institute for International Conflict Research. A political conflict is defined as "a positional difference, regarding values relevant to a society … between at least two assertive and directly involved actors" carried out through conflict measures beyond normal regulatory procedures. A highly violent political conflict (a "limited war" or "war", for definition see www.hiik.de/en/) is determined through five proxies: (i) weapons, (ii) personnel, (iii) casualties, (iv) refugees, and (v) IDPs and destruction. For more detailed information, see www.hiik.de/en/.

Of the 424 political conflicts in 2014, 223 involved the use of violence. This figure is subdivided into violent crises and highly violent conflicts. Highly violent conflicts include 25 limited wars and 21 wars.

Unlike UNHCR, when calculating the top refugee-producing countries, this report takes into account the number of refugees being assisted by UNRWA. As such, there is a discrepancy between the figure presented in this report (56 per cent of refugees come from 5 countries, based on 19.5 million refugees worldwide) and that presented by UNHCR in its report *Global Trends 2014: World at War* (53 per cent of refugees come from 3 countries, based on 14.4 million refugees under UNHCR's mandate).

Natural disasters in 2014

Figure 5. The data in this figure is for disasters associated with natural hazards. The total number of natural disasters does not include biological disasters, such as epidemics or insect infestations. The total number of disasters differs from the CRED EM-DAT *Annual Disaster Statistical Review 2014*, as it was downloaded directly from the database to showcase the most up-to-date information for 2014. The rest of the overall natural hazard information is sourced from the *Statistical Review*. To allow for ease of comparison between the graphs that map the occurrence and reporting of natural disasters, natural hazards are classified according to the natural disaster groupings used in ReliefWeb. These are earthquakes (including tsunamis), floods (including flash floods) and storms (including extra-tropical cyclone/winter storms, severe local storms, snow avalanches, storm surges and tropical cyclones).

Global landscape

Issues of increasing concern

Figure 6. Each baseline and predictive statistic is drawn from one or various sources. Users are encouraged to refer to the reference list and corresponding reports for the full descriptors and further statistics. The baseline statistic for poverty is for 2010. That is the last year for which the World Bank released poverty estimates (figures released in 2013).

UNHCR only has data for the number of Stateless people in 75 countries. This means data is not available for 50 per cent of the world's States. Stateless people from oPt are not included in statistical reporting. The Institute on Statelessness and Inclusion estimates 15 million Stateless people worldwide (UNHCR's 'at least 10 million', plus 1.5 million Stateless refugees, plus 3.5 million Stateless oPt refugees). The numbers under slavery and forced labour are derived from ILO's database and the Global Slavery Index.

Regional perspectives

Responding to natural disasters in the Asia-Pacific region

Figure 7. Data for these figures was provided by OCHA's Regional Office for Asia and the Pacific, in coordination with country offices.

Initial response and key immediate needs

Figure 8. Data for these figures was provided by OCHA's Regional Office for Asia and the Pacific, in coordination with country offices.

Middle East and North Africa: regional overview and country pages

Regional refugee-hosting countries in focus

Figures 9 and 10. Data for these figures was provided by OCHA's Regional Office for the Middle East and North Africa, in coordination with country offices. Data was completed by research at headquarters. Specific data sources and notations are as follows:

- **People affected by conflict**: these were calculated by adding the number of IDPs and refugees residing in a country. For the regional overview, 'people affected by conflict' include the sum of IDPs and refugees living in all countries under the purview of OCHA's Regional Office for the Middle East and North Africa (Afghanistan, Algeria, Bahrain, Egypt, Iran, Iraq, Jordan, Kuwait, Lebanon, Libya, Morocco, Oman, oPt, Pakistan, Saudi Arabia, Syria, Qatar, Tunisia, Turkey, United Arab Emirates and Yemen). Refugee figures reflect the number of refugees residing in a particular country, regardless of origin. The refugee figure includes both refugees covered under UNHCR's mandate and reported through UNHCR's statistical database plus Palestinian refugees under UNRWA's mandate. The latter is applicable to Jordan, Lebanon and Syria, who are hosts to Palestinian refugees as reported by UNRWA. IDP figures were provided by the Internal Displacement Monitoring Centre (IDMC). When IDMC's IDP figures are not available, UNHCR's figures are used. All numbers in detail are available for download through the report's dataset, **www.unocha.org/humanity360**.

- **Funding**: inter-agency appeal information from FTS was used to determine levels of financial humanitarian assistance. Data was retrieved on 1 August 2015. There may be some discrepancies as figures in FTS continue to be updated. While primarily focusing on inter-agency appeals, when data was available, the amount of funding requested and received for each country's portion of a regional response plan (RRP) is included in the calculation. The following countries were included in RRPs:

  - **2010 RRP for Iraqi refugees:** Jordan, Lebanon, Syria, Region (Egypt, Iran, Turkey and the Gulf States)
  - **2011 Libya RRP:** Libya, Egypt, Tunisia, Niger
  - **2013 Syria RRP:** Egypt, Iraq, Jordan, Lebanon, Turkey
  - **2014 Syria RRP:** Egypt, Iraq, Jordan, Lebanon, Turkey.

Funding received by country for the 2010 RRP for Iraqi refugees was not available. The 2011 Libya RRP showed the breakdown of funding per country. The total RRP is thus shown under Libya.

In an effort to provide as comprehensive a picture of humanitarian funding in the region, funding figures also show appeal-like processes reported through FTS, such as joint Government-UN appeals.

In the regional overview, funding figures were obtained from FTS and inter-agency appeal documents for countries/territories experiencing a humanitarian situation. These are Afghanistan, Egypt, Iraq, Jordan, Lebanon, Libya, oPt, Pakistan, Syria, Turkey and Yemen. The number of security incidents and aid workers affected were retrieved from the Aid Worker Security Database for these countries. There may be a discrepancy between figures reported to the Aid Worker Security Database and other security figures, such as those collected by the UN Department of Safety and Security with only focus on UN staff.

The funding gap represents the percentage difference between funding requested and funding received.

- Partnerships: the number of organizations participating in the inter-agency appeal denotes those humanitarian organizations (UN Agency, NGO, or Red Cross / Red Crescent) using the inter-agency appeal process/SRP to request funding for a specific project. These projects are included in FTS. The numbers of organization participating in inter-agency appeals were retrieved from FTS, with the exception of oPt. The OCHA oPt Country Office provided the number of humanitarian organizations participating in the CAP/SRP and these may differ from FTS. The numbers of international NGOs and national NGOs were reported by country teams to denote humanitarian organizations working to provide life-saving assistance and protection. Not all of these organization may participate in the inter-agency appeal.

Country-specific notations on data are as follows:

- **Jordan, Lebanon and Syria:** the refugee figures include refugees under UNHCR's mandate and Palestinian refugees under UNRWA's mandate.

- **Lebanon:** no IDP figures are shown for coherence with strategic response plans.

- **Pakistan:** for 2012 to 2014, the amount of people targeted and reached in the Agriculture Cluster is included in the Food Security Cluster.

- **Jordan:** the numbers of people targeted and reached reflect the number of Syrian refugees targeted and assisted in Jordan per sector. In addition, a further 650,000 Jordanians were targeted and assisted in 2014, and 500,000 Jordanians were targeted and assisted in

2013. 2015 figures are for the first quarter of 2015. Targets have been adjusted, given that the initial targets assumed 1 million refugees would be in the country by the end of 2013 and 800,000 by the end of 2014. Total refugee arrivals were fewer than expected.

- **Syria:** the numbers of people targeted and reached for each sector are derived from the SHARP's 'Sector Achievements' in 2013 and 2014. The number of national NGOs represents those that are authorised by the Syrian Government to partner with UN agencies. However, this does not mean that they all effectively work as partners with the UN, due to security-, access- and capacity-related reasons.

- **Turkey:** 2015 data current as of 31 March 2015.

- **Yemen:** 2014 protection figures include gender-based violence and child protection.

- **oPt:** 2013 figures as of midyear review. In 2014, 1.9 million people were reached through the SRP, with an additional 1.2 million reached through food distribution during the Gaza conflict.

Trends, challenges and opportunities

The cost of humanitarian assistance

Figure 11. The total number of people affected includes a sum of the total number of people affected by conflict globally and the total number of people affected by natural disasters in the world each year. The total number of people affected by conflict comprises the total number of IDPs (figures from *IDMC Global Estimates 2014*), asylum seekers and refugees (figures from UNHCR's 'Statistical Online Population Database'). The total number of people affected by natural disasters is sourced from CRED using the same criteria outlined in the technical note for figure 5. The total number of people targeted for assistance through inter-agency appeals is derived from OCHA midyear reviews.

The yearly peacekeeping budget was used as a measure for the cost of peacekeeping operations. Data on the peacekeeping budget comes from the UN Documents System, which comprises all types of official United Nations documentation, including resolutions of the General Assembly, Security Council, Economic and Social Council and the Trusteeship Council from 1946. The system is accessible at http://documents.un.org/.

The total amount of funding requested and received through inter-agency appeals is derived from FTS, specifically for appeals that have lasted at least a year.

These figures were adjusted for inflation (rates from the International Monetary Fund).

The costs for security of UN Field Operations are derived from UN budget documentation (programme planning) approved by the Fifth Committee for a given biennium. The costs are graphed on the year in which the biennium ends; for example, for the 2004-2005 fiscal biennium, the costs of security for field operations are plotted on the x-axis point for 2005. Budget documents are available at http://www.un.org/en/ga/fifth/.

Funding for development activities is larger than humanitarian assistance; for example, in 2103 funding for UN development system amounted to $16 billion (A/70/62). For the purposes of this figure, development funding is excluded from calculations to allow a direct comparison between peace operations and humanitarian assistance, especially as conflict is a key driver of the latter. For more information of development funding see Quadrennial Comprehensive Policy Review http://www.un.org/en/ecosoc/.

The length of peace operations was sourced from Einsiedel, Sebastian, Examining major recent trends in violent conflict, United Nations University, 2014. http://cpr.unu.edu/examining-major-recent-trends-inviolent-conflict.html.

The evolution of pooled funds

Figure 13. The word clouds only take into consideration the top five countries and sectors by levels of funding received. For a full list of countries funded and amount of funding disbursed (per country and sector), please consult the data set associated with this report (available through the Humanitarian Data Exchange).

Funding trends: where does the money come from?

Figure 14. For the purposes of this figure, appeal calculations for 2014 include the Typhoon Haiyan Strategic Response Plan and Zamboanga Crisis Response Plan. Funding for the flash appeals for the Bohol earthquake and Typhoon Hagupit (Ruby) are included under 'Contributions outside the appeal'. Appeal calculations for 2013 include the Mindanao Action Plan.

The humanitarian-development nexus in protracted crises

Figure 15. Funding per targeted person was calculated by dividing the appeal funding received per country from FTS by the number of targeted people. The number of targeted people was obtained from the midyear review of global humanitarian response overviews and previous versions

of appeals, e.g., consolidated appeal overviews, chapeau of humanitarian appeals and country-specific strategic response plans. If there were discrepancies in the figures provided in the global overview and in country-specific midyear reviews, preference was given to the country-specific plans. Data on development indicators (infant-mortality rate, literacy, cereal yield and access to improved water sources) is available from the World Bank's statistical database. Data for oil and energy prices was retrieved from the World Bank's Commodity Markets outlook. Data for food price index was retrieved from FAO.

Measuring impact: the case of Darfur

Figure 16. For the AU/UN Hybrid Operation in Darfur (UNAMID): the number of uniformed personnel includes military troops, police and the maximum number of formed police units authorized under the relevant Security Council resolutions, namely 1769 (2007), 1828 (2008), 1881 (2009), 1935 (2010), 2003 (2011), 2063 (2012), 2113 (2013) and 2173 (2014). Data on UNAMID's budget comes from the General Assembly's Fifth Committee's resolutions on financing UNAMID. Note that appropriations run from 1 July to 30 June.

Long-term trends in natural disasters, 2004-2014

Figure 17. Data retrieved from CRED EM-DAT on 1 October 2015. The number of inter-agency appeals includes flash appeals and other types of appeals, whereby there was a natural disaster component. The number of people targeted may be approximate. It is estimated based on original appeal documents, which have changed over time.

Long-term trends in conflict

Figure 18. In a deviation from the World Bank's geographic zones, this infographic uses the geographic zones defined in the Conflict Barometer of the Heidelberg Institute for International Conflict Research to reflect the research findings without compromising results. For a description of geographic zones and an explanation of conflict-intensity levels, please visit www.hiik.de/en/konfliktbarometer/. Data is available for previous years, however, data is only showcased from 2006 to coincide with the inclusion of the 'Distribution of all conflicts by region and intensity type' charts in the reports. This is in order to avoid a mistake when classifying previous information.

Disaster-related displacement and middle-income countries

Figure 20. Data on the number of disasters and overall people affected comes from CRED EM-DAT. Data on IDPs was provided by IDMC, based on its report *Global Estimates 2015: People displaced by disasters*. GDP per capita was retrieved from the World Bank's 'World Development Indicators Database'. The percentage of urban population was calculated by dividing estimates on the total number of urban dwellers by total population, based on data from the UN Statistics Division's Demographic Statistics 'Population by sex and urban/rural residence'. Data on urban population was not available for the Philippines and only for certain years for India.

When comparing the number of people affected with the number of IDPs in India in 2012, there is a statistical anomaly in that it is the only year where the proportions are inverted (i.e., more people displaced than affected). This could be due to the different methodology employed in data collection by IDMC and CRED EM-DAT. Excluding this statistical anomaly, the trend remains that in general, there are more people affected than displaced per country per year.

The impact of explosive weapons on civilian populations

The use of improvised explosive devices

Figures 21 and 22. Explosive weapons include manufactured ordnance such as aircraft bombs, mortars and rockets, as well as improvised explosive devices (IEDs). These infographics are based on data recorded by Action on Armed Violence (AOAV) between 2011 and 2014. During this period, AOAV recorded the impact of explosive weapons around the world using English language media sources. No claims are made that this data reflects every casualty or incident of explosive violence, but it reflects general trends and contexts in which civilians have been most at risk. AOAV uses an incident-based methodology adapted from the Robin Coupland and Nathan Taback model. Data on explosive violence incidents is gathered from English-language media reports on the following factors: date, time and location of the incident; the number and circumstances of people killed and injured; the weapon type; the reported user and target; the detonation method and whether displacement or damage to the location was reported. The narrow focus and methodology of AOAV's explosive violence monitoring mean that its civilian death and injury figures may be lower than the overall figures published by other agencies, such as the Office of the High

Commissioner for Human Rights. Comprehensive details about AOAV's methodology are at https://aoav.org.uk/explosiveviolence/methodology/.

Innovative tools for data coordination and collection

Figure 24. Digital responders have worked over the past year, often behind the scenes, to support the Ebola response in West Africa. Their efforts span data collection, map development, translations, emergency telecommunications and analysis, to name a few areas. A full storyboard highlighting the work of Digital Humanitarian Network-affiliated member organizations, while working towards disease elimination, is available here: http://digitalhumanitarians.com/DHNEbolaStoryboard/. OCHA hosts the OCHA KoBoToolbox server, https://kobo.humanitarianresponse.info. Software development and technical administration are managed by the KoBoToolbox project at the Harvard Humanitarian Initiative. Statistics on user accounts, number of deployed projects and data submissions are counted as of 14 August 2014 based on server database figures. Figures are as of 30 June 2015. The statistics do not include projects or data deleted by users and are thus slightly lower than the actual number.

Social media and humanitarian disasters: Typhoon Ruby

Figure 26. Source maps for geo-location of damage can be found here: http://maps.micromappers.org/2014/hagupit/tweets/ and http://maps.micromappers.org/2014/hagupit/images.

Perceptions about humanitarian action

Figure 27. Data is derived from the World Humanitarian Summit surveys conducted globally for diaspora, youth, and civil-military actors, and regionally for the WHS preparatory consultation for Eastern and Southern Africa; Europe and Others; Latin America and the Caribbean; Middle East and North Africa; South and Central Asia; and West and Central Africa.

Data sources and references

This report presents a compilation of data from various sources that are determined to be the most comprehensive and authoritative available. Much of the information is originally collected by Governments and compiled into global data sets by international organizations. Some information is collected directly by international organizations and research institutes, or gathered from other third-party sources.

Below are brief descriptions of the source organizations and the data they make available. Readers are directed to those organizations for additional data and information.

Active Learning Network for Accountability and Performance in Humanitarian Action (ALNAP). ALNAP conducts research on humanitarian practices and evaluation. www.alnap.org/

Action on Armed Violence (AOAV). AOAV carries out research, advocacy and field work in order to reduce the incidence and impact of global armed violence. AOAV works with communities affected by armed violence, removing the threat of weapons and supporting the recovery of victims and survivors. AOAV also carries out research and advocacy campaigns to strengthen international laws and standards on the availability and use of conventional weapons; to build recognition of the rights of victims and survivors of armed violence; and to research, understand and act on the root causes of armed violence. https://aoav.org.uk/

Centre for Research on the Epidemiology of Disasters International Disaster Database (CRED EM-DAT). The EM-DAT disaster database contains data on over 18,000 disasters from 1900. It is compiled from various sources, including United Nations agencies, NGOs, insurance companies, research institutes and press agencies. www.emdat.be/

Development Initiatives (DI). DI is an independent organization providing information and analysis that supports action on poverty. The Global Humanitarian Assistance programme at DI is a leading centre of research and analysis on international financing flows to situations of humanitarian crisis. www.devinit.org/ and *Global Humanitarian Assistance Report 2015* www.globalhumanitarianassistance.org/report/gha-report-2015. The Development Data Hub at DI is a data aggregator to provide a single source for financial resource-flow data alongside poverty, social and vulnerability indicators. http://devinit.org/#!/data

Digital Humanitarian Network (DHN). DHN leverages digital networks in support of humanitarian response. This network-of-networks aims to form a consortium of volunteer and technical communities and provide an interface between humanitarian organizations and these networks. Upon activation, DHN members can monitor real-time media and social media, geo-locate event and infrastructure data, create live crisis maps, undertake big-data analysis and tag/trace satellite imagery. http://digitalhumanitarians.com/

Feinstein International Center. This is a research and teaching centre based at Tufts University in the USA. The centre promoted the use of evidence and learning in operational and policy responses to protect and strengthen the lives, livelihoods and dignity of people affected by, or at risk of, humanitarian crises. http://fic.tufts.edu/ *Against the grain: the cereal trade in Darfur* (December 2014, http://fic.tufts.edu/assets/Cereal_trade_Darfur_V3_online3.pdf)

Financial Tracking Service - United Nations Office for the Coordination of Humanitarian Affairs (OCHA FTS). FTS is a global, real-time database that records all reported international humanitarian aid (including that for NGOs and the Red Cross/Red Crescent Movement), bilateral aid, in-kind aid and private donations. FTS features a special focus on consolidated appeals and flash appeals. All FTS data is provided by donors or recipient organizations. OCHA manages FTS. fts.unocha.org

Food and Agriculture Organization of the United Nations (FAO). FAO works to raise levels of nutrition, improve agricultural productivity, improve the lives of rural populations and contribute to the growth of the world economy. It collates and disseminates a wide range of food–and-agricultural statistics. www.fao.org/economic/ess/ and *The State of Food Insecurity in the World 2014* www.fao.org/3/a-i4037e.pdf

Global Slavery Index. The Global Slavery Index provides a country-by-country estimate of the number of people living in modern slavery today. It is a tool to help citizens, NGOs, businesses and public officials to understand the size of the problem, existing responses and contributing factors so they can build sound policies to end modern slavery. http://www.globalslaveryindex.org/

Harvard Humanitarian Initiative (HHI). HHI is a Harvard University-wide centre that provides expertise in public health, medicine, social science, management and other disciplines to promote evidence-based approaches to humanitarian assistance. hhi.harvard.edu/

Heidelberg Institute for International Conflict Research (HIIK). HIIK is an independent and interdisciplinary association located at the Department of Political Science at the University of Heidelberg, Germany. HIIK is a leading authority in researching and disseminating knowledge on the emergence, course and settlement of inter-State, intra-State and sub-political conflicts. hiik.de/en/index.html and Conflict Barometer 2014 http://www.hiik.de/en/konfliktbarometer/

Humanitarian Data Exchange (HDX). HDX aims to make humanitarian data easy to find and use for analysis. Three elements—a repository, analytics and standards—will eventually combine into an integrated data platform. https://data.hdx.rwlabs.org/

Humanitarian Outcomes – Aid Worker Security Database (AWSD). AWSD records major incidents of violence against aid workers, with incident reports from 1997 through to the present. aidworkersecurity.org/

Index for Risk Management (InforRM). InfoRM is a global, open-source risk assessment for humanitarian crises and disasters. It can support decisions about prevention, preparedness and response. InfoRM covers 191 countries and includes natural and human hazards. It combines about 50 different indicators that measure hazards, vulnerability and capacity. http://www.inform-index.org/

Institute for Economics and Peace (IEP). IEP is a think tank dedicated to developing metrics to analyse peace and quantify its economic value. It does this by developing global and national indices, calculating the economic cost of violence, analysing country-level risk and understanding positive peace. IEP produced the annual Global Peace Index, a statistical analysis of the state of peace in 162 countries, outlining trends in peace and conflict, the economic cost of violence, and an assessment of the attitudes, structures and institutions that sustain peaceful societies. http://economicsandpeace.org/ and Global Peace Index 2015. http://www.visionofhumanity.org/

Inter-agency appeal documents and strategic response plans – OCHA. The Humanitarian Planning Cycle brings aid organizations together to jointly plan, coordinate, implement and monitor their response to natural disasters and complex emergencies. The appeal process results in appeal documents, which contain information on the number of people affected by emergencies, their needs and the funding required to respond to those needs. OCHA facilitates the appeal process. www.humanitarianresponse.info

Internal Displacement Monitoring Centre (IDMC). IDMC, part of the Norwegian Refugee Council, monitors and analyses internal displacement caused by conflict,

generalized violence, human rights violations and natural-hazard-induced disasters to provide policymakers across the humanitarian and development fields with independent information and analysis. www.internal-displacement.org/ and Global Estimates 2014: People displaced by disasters. www.internal-displacement.org/publications/2014/global-estimates-2014-people-displaced-by-disasters/

International Labour Organization (ILO). ILO aims to promote rights at work, encourage decent employment opportunities, enhance social protection and strengthen dialogue on work-related issues. www.ilo.org/ and Global Employment Trends for Youth 2013 www.ilo.org/global/research/global-reports/global-employment-trends/youth/2013/WCMS_212423/ lang--en/index.htm

Intergovernmental Panel on Climate Change (IPCC). IPCC is the international body for assessing the science related to climate change. It was established to provide policymakers with regular assessments of the scientific basis of climate change, its impacts and future risks, and options for adaptation and mitigation. http://ipcc-wg2.gov/AR5/

International Organization for Migration (IOM). IOM helps to ensure the orderly and humane management of migration, to promote international cooperation on migration issues, to assist in the search for practical solutions to migration problems, and to provide humanitarian assistance to migrants in need, be they refugees, displaced people or other uprooted people. www.iom.int/cms/en/sites/iom/home.html and Fatal Journeys, Tracking Lives Lost during Migration. http://www.iom.int/files/live/sites/iom/files/pbn/docs/Fatal-Journeys-Tracking-Lives-Lost-during-Migration-2014.pdf

International Peace Institute – Global Observatory. The Global Observatory provides timely analysis on peace and security issues by experts, journalists and policymakers. It includes a Catalogue of Indices, where more than 60 indices and indicators have been categorized into eight themes and visualized into an interactive map. http://theglobalobservatory.org/ and http://theglobalobservatory.org/2015/04/catalogue-indices-maps/

International Telecommunications Union (ITU). ITU is the United Nations specialized agency for information and communication technologies (ICTs). ITU allocates global radio spectrum and satellite orbits, develops the technical standards that ensure networks and technologies interconnect, and strives to improve access to ICTs to underserved communities worldwide. www.itu.int

KoBoToolbox. KoBoToolbox is an integrated set of tools for building forms and collecting interview responses. It was built by the Harvard Humanitarian Initiative for easy and reliable use in difficult field settings, such as humanitarian emergencies or post-conflict environments. It is hosted and supported by OCHA and can be used without limitations by any humanitarian organization. https://kobo.humanitarianresponse.info/

Millennium Development Goals Report – Department of Economic and Social Affairs, United Nations. This annual report presents the most comprehensive global assessment of progress to date, based on data provided by a large number of international organizations within and outside the United Nations system. The aggregate figures in the report provide an overview of regional progress under the eight goals, and they are a convenient way to track advances over time. http://www.un.org/millenniumgoals/reports.shtml

Munich Re. Munich Re combines primary insurance and re-insurance, specializing in risk management. Its primary insurance operations are concentrated mainly in the ERGO Insurance Group, one of the major insurance groups in Germany and Europe. www.munichre.com/en/homepage/index.html

Norwegian Refugee Council (NRC). NRC is an independent, humanitarian, non-profit NGO. It provides assistance, protection and durable solutions to refugees and internally displaced persons worldwide. http://www.nrc.no/

Organisation for Economic Co-operation and Development's Development Assistance Committee (OECD DAC). OECD DAC is a forum for selected OECD Member States to discuss issues surrounding aid, development and poverty reduction. OECD DAC provides comprehensive data on the volume, origin and types of aid and other resource flows to over 180 aid recipients. www.oecd.org/dac/stats/idsonline

Oxfam. Oxfam is an international confederation of 17 organizations working with partners and local communities in more than 90 countries that work to create lasting solutions against "the injustice of poverty". To achieve its purpose, Oxfam uses a combination of sustainable development programmes, public education, campaigns, advocacy and humanitarian assistance. https://www.oxfam.org/

PreventionWeb. This is a participatory web platform for the disaster risk reduction (DRR) community. It facilitates an understanding of DRR and professionals' work in this area by providing current news and views on the topic and tools for exchange and collaboration. http://www.preventionweb.net/english/

Qatar Computing Research Institute (QCRI). QCRI conducts innovative, multidisciplinary applied computing research that addresses national priorities by enhancing the quality of life for citizens, enabling broader scientific discoveries and making local businesses more competitive globally. http://www.qcri.com/

ReliefWeb. ReliefWeb provides reliable disaster and crisis updates and analysis to humanitarians so they can make informed decisions and plan effective assistance. http://labs.reliefweb.int/

Standby Taskforce Team (SBTF). The SBTF is a global network of volunteers who collaborate online in the immediate aftermath of a natural disaster. The network draws from the latest technologies available, such as crisis mapping, artificial intelligence disaster response and other open-source solutions, with an aim to streamline and scale social media monitoring, and provide verification, geo-location and analysis in support of crisis response. http://blog.standbytaskforce.com/

United Nations Central Emergency Response Fund (CERF). CERF is a humanitarian fund that was established by the United Nations General Assembly in 2006 to enable more timely and reliable humanitarian assistance to people affected by natural disasters and armed conflicts. www.unocha.org/cerf/

United Nations Children's Fund (UNICEF). UNICEF provides long-term humanitarian and development assistance to children and mothers in developing countries. It tracks progress through data collection and analysis and updates global databases. www.unicef.org/statistics/

United Nations Department of Economic and Social Affairs (DESA). DESA promotes development and works on issues including poverty reduction, population, macroeconomic policy, development finance and sustainable development. It generates and compiles a wide range of data and information on development issues. http://unstats.un.org/unsd/, *World Urbanization Prospects, 2014 Revision* www.un.org/en/development/desa/publications/2014-revision-world-urbanization-prospects.html, *International Migration Report 2013* www.un.org/en/development/desa/population/publications/migration/migration-report-2013.shtml, *The World Population Prospects: 2015 Revision* https://www.un.org/development/desa/publications/world-population-prospects-2015-revision.html, *World Economic Situation and Prospects 2015* https://www.un.org/development/desa/publications/wesp-2015-2.html#more-944)

United Nations Development Programme (UNDP). UNDP supports countries to reach their development objectives and internationally agreed goals, including the Millennium Development Goals. It collects, analyses and disseminates human development data, including through the preparation of the Human Development Index and its components. http://hdr.undp.org/en/statistics/ and the Human Development Reports http://hdr.undp.org/en

United Nations Education, Scientific and Cultural Organization (UNESCO). UNESCO strives to build networks among nations by mobilizing for education, building intercultural understanding through the protection of heritage and support for cultural diversity, pursuing scientific cooperation and protecting freedom of expression. http://en.unesco.org/

United Nations Office for the Coordination of Humanitarian Affairs (OCHA). OCHA is responsible for bringing together humanitarian actors to ensure a coherent response to emergencies. OCHA's mission is to mobilize and coordinate effective and principled humanitarian action in partnership with national and international actors, advocate the rights of people in need, promote preparedness and prevention, and facilitate sustainable solutions. http://www.unocha.org/, http://www.unocha.org/about-us/publications, OCHA Regional Office for Middle East and North Africa http://www.unocha.org/romena and OCHA Regional Office for Asia and the Pacific http://www.unocha.org/roap

United Nations Office for Disaster Risk Reduction (UNISDR). UNISDR is the focal point in the United Nations system to ensure coordination and synergies among DRR activities of the United Nations system and regional organizations and activities in socioeconomic and humanitarian fields (GA resolution 56/195). UNISDR also supports the implementation, follow-up and review of the *Sendai Framework for Disaster Risk Reduction 2015-2030* (Sendai Framework). http://www.unisdr.org/ and *Global Assessment Report on Disaster Risk Reduction* http://www.preventionweb.net/english/hyogo/gar/2015/en/home/

United Nations High Commissioner for Refugees (UNHCR). UNHCR is mandated to lead and coordinate international action to protect refugees and resolve refugee problems worldwide. It provides data and statistics about people of concern to UNHCR, including refugees, asylum seekers, returned refugees, the internally displaced and stateless people. www.unhcr.org/statistics and *The Global Report 2013* www.unhcr.org/pages/49c3646c278.html

United Nations Human Settlements Programme (UN-Habitat). UN-Habitat promotes socially and environmentally sustainable towns and cities. It collects, analyses and disseminates human-settlements statistics. www.unhabitat.org/stats/

United Nations Office on Drugs and Crime (UNODC). UNODC is mandated to assist Member States in their struggle against illicit drugs, crime and terrorism. UNODC works through field-based technical cooperation projects; research and analytical work to increase knowledge and understanding of drugs and crime issues; and normative work to assist States in the ratification and implementation of the relevant international treaties. www.unodc.org/ and www.unodc.org/unodc/en/data-and-analysis/statistics/index.html

United States Agency for International Development (USAID). USAID is the lead US Government agency that works to end extreme global poverty and enable resilient, democratic societies. USAID works in over 100 countries to promote shared economic prosperity, strengthen democracy, protect human rights, improve global health, advance food security, further education, help in conflict recovery and provide humanitarian assistance. www.usaid.gov

UN-Water. UN-Water is the United Nations inter-agency coordination mechanism for all freshwater- and sanitation-related matters. *World Water Development Report 2014* www.unwater.org/publications/publications-detail/en/c/218614/

UN Women. UN Women was established in 2010 as the United Nations entity for gender equality and the empowerment of women. UN Women aims to support intergovernmental bodies, such as the Commission on the Status of Women, in their formulation of policies, global standards and norms; help Member States to implement these standards and to forge effective partnerships with civil society; and lead and coordinate the UN's work on gender equality. http://www.unwomen.org/ and *Beijing Declaration and Platform for Action* http://www.unwomen.org/~/media/headquarters/attachments/sections/csw/pfa_e_final_web.pdf?v=1&d=20150303T234153

World Bank. The World Bank provides financial and technical assistance to developing countries. It provides access to a comprehensive set of data about all aspects of development. It also works to help developing countries improve the capacity, efficiency and effectiveness of national statistical systems.

http://data.worldbank.org/, *PovcalNet* http://iresearch.worldbank.org/PovcalNet/index.htm and *World Development Indicators*
http://data.worldbank.org/products/wdi

World Food Programme (WFP). WFP is the United Nations frontline agency mandated to combat global hunger. It publishes data, including on the number of people it targets and reaches with food assistance, food-aid flows and food and commodity prices.
www.wfp.org/content/wfp-achievements-2013

World Health Organization (WHO). WHO is the directing and coordinating authority for health within the United Nations system. It provides access to data and analyses for monitoring the global health situation, including through its Global Health Observatory. http://apps.who.int/gho/data/

World Humanitarian Summit (WHS). The WHS is an initiative of the United Nations Secretary-General. It is the first global summit on humanitarian action of this size and scope, and it will be held in Istanbul on 23 and 24 May 2016. Its goal is to bring the global community together to commit to new ways of working together to save lives and reduce hardship around the globe.
https://www.worldhumanitariansummit.org/

OCHA Policy Publications

OCHA Policy Studies

- World Humanitarian Data and Trends (Annual)
- Leaving no one behind: humanitarian effectiveness in the age of the Sustainable Development Goals
- Saving Lives Today and Tomorrow: Managing the Risk of Humanitarian Crises
- Humanitarianism in the Network Age including World Humanitarian Data and Trends 2012
- Coordination to Save Lives - History and Emerging Challenges
- To Stay and Deliver: Good practice for humanitarians in complex security environments
- OCHA Aide Memoire
- Safety and Security for National Humanitarian Workers

OCHA Occasional Policy Series

The objective of the series is to stimulate a debate and dialogue, or to generate feedback, views and advice. These publications area available online through **http://www.unocha.org/about-us/publications**.

#1   Global Challenges and their Impact on International Humanitarian Action, *January 2010*

#2   Climate Change and Humanitarian Action: Key Emerging Trends and Challenges, *August 2009*

#3   Energy Security and Humanitarian Action: Key Emerging Trends and Challenges, *September 2010*

#4   Water Scarcity and Humanitarian Action: Key Emerging Trends and Challenges, *September 2010*

#5   OCHA Evaluations Synthesis Report 2010, *February 2011*

#6   OCHA and Slow-onset Emergencies, *April 2011*

#7   Cross-Border Operations: A Legal Perspective, *forthcoming, 2015*

#8   Security Council Practice on the Protection of Civilians: Analysis of Key Normative Trends, *2014*

#9   Humanitarian Innovation: The State of the Art, *2014*

#10 Help from Above: Unmanned Aerial vehicles in Humanitarian Response, *2014*

#11 Humanitarianism in the Age of Cyber Warfare: The Principled and Secure Use of Information in Humanitarian Emergencies, *2014*

#12 Hashtag Standards for Emergencies, *2014*

#13 Interoperability: humanitarian action in a shared space, *July 2015*

#14 Shrinking the supply chain: Hyperlocal manufacturing and 3D printing in humanitarian response, *July 2015*

#15 An end in sight: multi-year planning to meet and reduce humanitarian needs in protracted crises, *July 2015*

#16 Crowdfunding for emergencies, *August 2015*

Join us

 unocha.org

 reliefweb.int

 data.hdx.rwlabs.org

 worldhumanitariansummit.org

 fts.unocha.org

 @fts.unocha & @ochapolicy

 facebook.com/unocha

 instagram.com/un_ocha

 medium.com/@UNOCHA

youtube.com/ochafilms

This publication was developed by the Policy
Analysis and Innovation Section of OCHA's Policy
Development and Studies Branch.

Managing Editor: Lilian Barajas
Researchers: Brittany Card, Paulina Odame
Design and layout: Broadley Design
Photo credits: OCHA, UNHCR

OCHA wishes to thank data-source organizations
and acknowledge the contributions of staff and
partners in preparing and reviewing this document.

For more information, please contact:

Policy Development and Studies Branch (PDSB)
United Nations Office for the Coordination
of Humanitarian Affairs (OCHA)

E-mail: ochapolicy@un.org